07
O
Xc
u

2

25.

Covent

BATTLE
for the SKIES

BATTLE
for the SKIES

Michael Paterson

David & Charles

A DAVID & CHARLES BOOK
David & Charles is a subsidiary of F+W (UK) Ltd.,
an F+W Publications Inc. company

First published in the UK in 2004

Distributed in North America
by F+W Publications, Inc.
4700 East Galbraith Road
Cincinnati, OH 45236
1-800-289-0963

A catalogue record for this book is available from
the British Library.

ISBN 0 7153 1815 2 hardback

Printed in Singapore by KHL Printing Co Pte Ltd
for David & Charles
Brunel House   Newton Abbot   Devon

Commissioning Editor   Neil Baber
Desk Editor   Lewis Birchon
Designer   Jodie Lystor
Production Controller   Jennifer Campbell

Visit our website at www.davidandcharles.co.uk

David & Charles books are available from all good bookshops;
alternatively you can contact our Orderline on (0)1626 334555
or write to us at FREEPOST EX2 110, David & Charles Direct,
Newton Abbot, TQ12 4ZZ (no stamp required UK mainland).

CONTENTS

INTRODUCTION

The air war of 1939–45 is unique in history because of its scale. Never before, and never afterward, did such multitudes of men fly such immense numbers of aircraft in combat over such great stretches of the globe. Never, before or since, have such enormous amounts of bombs wrought such widespread destruction.

Before the war began, the horror of aerial bombing had been anticipated by generals, governments and the public. Several European cities had experienced air raids during the Great War, but it was taken for granted that future attacks would be bigger and deadlier. The Spanish Civil War of 1936–39 involved pilots from two major powers – Germany and the Soviet Union – and demonstrated the capabilities of a modern air force. Madrid and Guernica, bombed by Fascist forces, symbolized the apocalypse to come.

Aerial bombardment proved even more terrible than had been foreseen yet it never – at least until the atomic bombs were unleashed on Japan – completely annihilated a city or a country, or cowed an entire population into surrender.

It had been believed in some quarters that air forces could fight, and decide, the conflict by themselves – that whatever the terrors of bombing it would at least prevent a recurrence of attritional trench warfare. Events were to prove otherwise. There were still to be huge land campaigns, sea battles, clashes of armour, guerrilla operations, exhaustive sieges, stalemate and attrition. In the West, the war's decisive event was a seaborne landing. Aircraft, with their guns and rockets, bombs and paratroops, did not win or lose the war on their own.

The roles they played from beginning to end were, however, crucial. The Luftwaffe made Blitzkrieg possible and led German armies across Poland, Western Europe and Russia. The Nazi juggernaut was halted at the Channel by RAF Fighter Command. The sole effective means of hitting back at Germany in the war's early years was provided by Bomber Command and by the US Army Air Force, whose constantly-escalating offensive destabilized, though did not destroy, German communications, industry and morale. In every theatre of war – Europe, the Mediterranean, North Africa, Russia and the Far East – aircraft provided reconnaissance and supplies as well as support for troops on the ground. At sea they vastly extended the operational range of navies and fought entire battles with scarcely the need for ships to engage. It was aircraft that delivered German paratroops to Holland and Crete and brought their Allied counterparts to Arnhem. They dropped supplies to Chindits in Burma and to the Americans surrounded in Bastogne. They failed in the impossible task of supplying the garrison at Stalingrad, thus sealing Hitler's fate in the East. They brought an end to the war by destroying Japan's will to resist through the obliteration of Hiroshima and Nagasaki.

In Russia and the Pacific there was no mutual respect between fliers on the opposing sides, and in the West there was no noticeable empathy between Allied and Axis bomber crews. Among those who flew fighters, however, there continued the notion begun in 1914 that the air war was a gentleman's war. Pilots had more in common with each other than with the civilians in their respective countries. They ran the same risks, admired each others' skill and took a professional interest in the technical details of each others' craft. Their targets were overwhelmingly military rather than economic so that the term 'air-gangster', used by both sides against bomber crews, did not apply.

Though some German pilots were undoubtedly National Socialists and therefore ideologically motivated, there was no airborne equivalent of the SS to dishonour the German effort with fanaticism and atrocity, as happened in the land war. Mistreatment of a downed opponent by either air force was rare. More commonly a captured flier might be invited to lunch, visited in his cell, presented with drinks and cigarettes, or even allowed to examine an enemy aircraft before the journey to prison-camp. The postwar friendships that often developed among former enemy pilots, some of which are reflected in the stories that follow, testify to the strength of this feeling.

The opportunity to use material from the unique collection of pilot profiles assembled by the Military Gallery in Wendover has meant that the characters represented in this book are some of the most famous, successful and celebrated airmen of the war. But this does not tell the whole story. Though the memories of aces can make exciting reading, not every pilot was an ace; not all aircrew were pilots, and not all members of an air force were aircrew. To broaden the scope of the book, therefore, accounts have been added by some of those who were on the ground, whether as maintenance crew, off-duty personnel or simply witnesses, as well as material from other theatres of operations.

Without control of the skies, the armies and the fleets could not have gained the victories they did. This book is dedicated to those who flew and fought on both sides in that singular and heroic generation.

1

MAN AND MACHINE

They were always an elite, the men – and the very few women – who flew in combat. Only a particular type, unknown until the twentieth century, could engage the enemy while defying the force of gravity. In their flimsy, canvas and plywood craft, with cockpits open to the elements and in many cases no parachute, the flyers of World War I seem like heroes just for going aloft.

For those susceptible to the challenge and romance of the air, there were glorious compensations for the risk of a fiery plunge to earth: the sense of freedom enjoyed by those who soared above the battlefields; the pleasure of the flying itself; the excitement of individual combat; and the mutual respect often shown by opponents. The early fighter pilots saw in themselves the revival of medieval chivalry combined with state-of-the-art technology, and to the public imagination this proved an irresistible combination.

The ones who survived and succeeded in shooting down enemy machines began to be referred to as 'aces'. To qualify for what was becoming an exclusive brotherhood a pilot needed to have made ten 'kills'. The number was subsequently lowered to five, but the term – and the notion of measuring excellence by opponents destroyed – has lasted ever since.

The young men who would fly a new generation of combat aircraft more than two decades later grew up in the afterglow of this glamour. But while fighting, with its risks and excitements, was over, aviation was still a thrilling adventure.

Huge strides were made in technology and design. Aircraft became bigger. They could fly higher and faster, carry more cargo and convey passengers in greater comfort. Oceans, deserts and continents were crossed by intrepid pilots who broke records for speed and distance. Air shows, flying and gliding clubs, hobby magazines and scale models brought the romance of flight within reach of every schoolboy.

Many who flew on both sides in World War II would remember the moment when, for them, the adventure began, and the motivations of boys of different nationalities and cultures were often strikingly similar.

MARION E CARL, USMC

From the time I first saw an aeroplane in the air I wanted to be an aviator.

ROD SMITH, RCAF

When I was five I saw a biplane flying from a field near Regina in Canada where I lived. It broke its undercarriage at the moment it lifted off and belly-landed later in a cloud of dust. Aeroplanes captivated me ever after.

A similar mishap inspired a future Luftwaffe flyer:

FRIEDRICH OBLESER, LUFTWAFFE

I decided to become a pilot in 1931 at eight years of age, when a Junkers F-13 postal aircraft made an emergency landing in a meadow near my home. With my father in charge of its security, I was given a guided tour of the aircraft by the pilot, which left me smitten. From that day onwards, aircraft and flying have dominated my life.

Some were driven by hero-worship:

JOHNNIE JOHNSON, RAF

At school I always wanted to become an RAF fighter pilot, and I was inspired by legendary aces of the First World War – Ball, Boelcke, von Richthofen, Mannock and McCudden.

ADOLF GALLAND, LUFTWAFFE

Fascinated by the adventures of the world's great pioneer aviators and stimulated by the exploits of combat pilots, I began my career in aviation, flying gliders at the tender age of 15.

While for others it was a matter of family tradition:

ROBIN OLDS, USAAF

I grew up with combat aviation in my blood, my father having served as a pilot in France in World War I. He was responsible as much as anything else for my burning desire to be a pilot.

One of the great Luftwaffe aces received a parental shove of a different kind:

ERICH HARTMANN, LUFTWAFFE

My mother was a keen aviation enthusiast and taught me to fly gliders when I was only 14.

Those with an early and passionate sense of vocation were, however, a minority. Many others had come to flying as a weekend hobby or a civilian profession and had found themselves, on the outbreak of war, in possession of skills that were much in demand.

RUSS BANNOCK, RCAF

After high school in Edmonton . . . I went to work for a mining company in Yellowknife, and in my spare time I learned to fly and obtained a commercial pilot's licence. On 9 September, 1939, I joined the RAF as a Pilot Officer . . .

RED SOMERVILLE, RCAF

. . . in the late summer of 1939 I flew commercially in the Toronto area, mostly joy-riding passengers on weekends.

He was later to be a distinguished Mosquito pilot.

Aware of the worsening international situation, many young men in Britain and North America enlisted in auxiliary air force units or university training schemes.

CHRIS FOXLEY-NORRIS, RAF

In 1936 I was commissioned in the Reserve Air Force Officers through the Oxford University Air Squadron, and was called to active service shortly before the outbreak of war . . .

Not everyone had this option, however. Such was the appeal of flying that these units were frequently oversubscribed.

SANDY JOHNSTONE, RAF

There was always much competition to get into the squadrons of the Auxiliary Air Force and I was proud to be invited to join 602 (City of Glasgow) Squadron . . . as it was the original squadron of that very exclusive force.

For their counterparts in Germany there was no need to worry about exclusiveness, for in 1935 Hitler reintroduced conscription. Prior to that, with Germany forbidden under the terms of the Versailles Treaty from having an air force, pilots had to be schooled with the utmost secrecy. Many learned the basics through seemingly innocuous local glider-clubs and then undertook advanced training in the Soviet Union, with which Germany had clandestinely made an agreement in the 1920s.

HANNES TRAUTLOFT, LUFTWAFFE

My military training began in secret. As a disguised 19-year-old officer cadet, I began flying training in April 1931 at Schleissheim near Munich. After a year . . . I was sent to Russia, with nine others from my course, for pre-military fighter pilot training. This top-

secret course was conducted by German officers using a selection
of biplanes . . .

He added that, to keep up the pretence . . .

I officially became a soldier in October 1932 to train as an infantry
officer. I received civilian refresher courses during my leave and
later, as a disguised Lieutenant, spent two years as an instructor at
the Fighter Pilots' School . . .

Once Germany had removed this cloak of secrecy, the Luftwaffe's ranks
were quickly filled with both volunteers and draftees. Once again, those
with relevant skills were eagerly sought.

ERICH RUDORFFER, LUFTWAFFE

Having initiated my training as a commercial pilot, I was conscripted
into the Luftwaffe in 1938 to fly fighters . . .

Demonstrating that by no means all Luftwaffe pilots were burning with
National Socialist idealism, he looked ahead to the coming conflict and
declared that he was:

Happy to be a fighter pilot since, confident of my own ability, I felt
that it gave me the best chance of surviving the war. I certainly
didn't want to drop bombs!

Most of those who joined the air forces of their countries did so once
hostilities had broken out. Some chose what they saw as the most exciting,
or most valuable form of service, for the air war was expected by both sides
to be the crucial field of action. Others, with the memory of the Flanders
trenches still vivid, wanted to ensure that they had no part in the ground
war. There was no shortage of young men who dreamed of flying, even in the
hazardous conditions of conflict. Sometimes this desire resulted in sacrifices:

OMER LEVESQUE, RCAF

When World War II began I was a Second Lieutenant in . . . the Royal 22nd Regiment but resigned my commission after the retreat to Dunkirk and entered the RCAF as an Aircraftman Second Class because it was the only way I could pursue my dream of becoming a pilot.

Two other North Americans had very personal reasons for enlisting. Both were involved with the sinking of the *Athenia*, a British passenger liner torpedoed on the first day of the war.

HUGH GODEFROY, RCAF

In the fall of 1939 I was very upset when a young girlfriend of mine was missing from the SS *Athenia* – sunk by a U-boat in the Atlantic. I immediately applied to join the Royal Canadian Air Force . . .

Jim Goodson's motivation was even more personal – he was on board.

JIM GOODSON, RAF

After helping the crew in rescuing the passengers, I slithered down a rope, swam to a lifeboat and was finally picked up by a Norwegian tanker which took me to Galway in Ireland. I had one goal: to become a fighter pilot in the RAF.

Once the fighting was under way, a whole generation of schoolboys was inspired by the deeds they witnessed over Britain's cities.

MICHAEL BEETHAM, RAF

My father was serving in the army in Portsmouth and I spent the summer holidays of 1940 there – and got a front-line view of the Battle of Britain as the Spitfires and Hurricanes tackled the German bombers raiding the important naval base. I decided then and there to join the RAF and, as soon as I was 18, in May 1941, I volunteered.

He ended his career as a Marshal of the Royal Air Force.

Those who made this choice can have been in no doubt that a hard road lay ahead of them. Aircrew training could take up to three years, and thus they might not be in time to participate in the war at all. If they did, they had to be able to call on a whole range of personal resources. The German historian Hans Ring summed these up as:

'Above-average intelligence, medical fitness . . . perfect eyesight, lengthy training – and above all, luck.'

Some men chose to fly fighters or bombers, others were assigned according to the needs of the moment or to marked qualities – their suitability to work alone or as part of a close-knit crew, an ability to navigate, shoot or operate communications. Fighter pilots were seen in every air force as more dashing. This observation by a Russian woman who was herself a combat tt suggests that even their 'body language' set the two types apart:

KATERINA FEDOTOVA, SOVIET AIR FORCE

We always said that we [the members of her female squadron] could tell one sort of male pilot from another without even speaking to him. The bomber pilots walked in a particular way. They were rather slow and deliberate and even ponderous-looking sometimes. The fighter pilots walked with more swagger and style and they had a certain nerviness about their whole bearing. Well, we believed we could tell them apart that way, anyway.

A fighter pilot must be an individualist. Though part of a team, and required to fly and fight in formation, he ultimately had only his own skill to rely upon. He had to be confident, for a timid flyer, unwilling to push his machine to its limits, would not last long.

He needed excellent vision, for a distant speck in his mirror could, within seconds, become an enemy aircraft on his tail. He had to have physical stamina, for even a few minutes of combat would leave him exhausted and drenched in sweat as he wrenched and teased the controls of his machine. Most demanding of all, he must be able to aim and fire at hurtling, spinning, weaving targets while his own craft banked and twisted at hundreds of miles an hour. As the American aviation authors Raymond Toliver and Trevor Constable point out, success and survival depended more on good shooting than good flying.

He must also have exceptional mental toughness, for he must cope with split-second decisions, run the risk of blackouts while turning tight circles, shrug off the horror of friends suddenly and violently killed and deal with damage to himself and his aircraft. With his plane disabled and his clothing on fire he might face the prospect of bailing out (often his first experience of using a parachute) with the choppy waters of the Channel, or the Pacific, thousands of feet below.

The qualities required by those who served in bombers were no less exceptional. The ability to fly, manoeuvre and shoot were just as vital, but a different type of courage was needed by those who flew lengthy missions over enemy territory, whether the target was London or Berlin or Tokyo. While a fighter dogfight might last seconds and a sortie an hour or two, a bombing mission from East Anglia to Berlin and back would normally take eight to ten hours. It needed a steady nerve to deal with the build-up to a raid – the briefing, the seemingly-endless waiting and, when airborne, the further long hours in the freezing stratosphere, flying through curtains of anti-aircraft fire.

Once the objective was reached, there were the moments of intense concentration as the aircraft was aligned on the target and its bombs released. There was the sight of other aircraft, stricken and plunging into the sea of fire below, the thought of the return journey across hundreds of miles of land and water, harassed by flak and fighters for much of the way, and, if one survived, the knowledge that it would all have to be done again the following night. One survivor listed the range of feelings common to men in this situation:

DONALD H SMITH, USAAF

Fear, at some level of intensity . . . perhaps most obvious in the

locker area as we donned our flying clothes prior to a mission,
usually covered by an expression of stoicism or by coarse army
humour . . .

The nervous moments, early into a mission, sometimes seemed surreal:

Feelings of adventure and curiosity as we headed into our first
mission . . . Difficulty believing those first black puffs of exploding
88mm shells were from enemy gunners attempting to kill us . . .
Foreboding preceding other missions. A sick feeling of 'how did
I get myself into such a situation?' on the approach to a target
. . . Some knowledge that there was no guardian angel – 'it' could
happen to anyone.

The price of belonging to the fraternity of the air was high.

* * *

To those who flew in both fighters and bombers, their planes were more
than mere wood and metal. The countless hours of training, flying and
fighting in an aircraft created a relationship that was intimate and
personal – though not necessarily affectionate.

LEONARD KENT, RAF

I flew Fairey Battles, but on only one sortie, thank God! This aircraft
was underpowered and proved a disaster.

More commonly, however, pilots and crews developed a fondness for their
aircraft akin to that of a cavalryman for his horse.

NATHANIEL FLEKSER, SOUTH AFRICAN AIR FORCE

We had developed a symbiotic relationship – even a love affair.
I thought of a manoeuvre and she executed it. She responded

to my gentlest touch and my most violent contortions with equal
sensitivity. And she always brought me back . . .

Bombers could also have personalities.

DONALD H SMITH, USAAF

[Our B-17] had a reputation as being a troublesome bird, hard to fly,
but always making it back.

Some accounts even imply that an aircraft had a mind of its own. An
American ball-turret gunner described a bomber's flight after the crew
had bailed out of their stricken plane near the Swiss frontier:

GEORGE HINTZ, USAAF

Incredibly, our severely damaged and now pilotless B-17 flew on
and made a respectable crash-landing in a forest clearing at the
southern end of the Baldegger Lake, Switzerland.

These feelings were based on trust in an aircraft's technical abilities
as well as the extent to which crews would rely on the accuracy of its
firepower, the strength of its air-frame and its endurance of continuous
punishment. Nothing led pilots to love a plane more than the notion
that, even when shot full of holes, it brought them home. A plane that
could not be relied on for speed, manoeuvrability or armament was worse
than useless.

Yet any notion of a plane as a safe and solid flying pillbox would not
have lasted long. Aircrew and ground-crews would, in a normal tour of
duty, have seen dozens of aircraft perish – often in horrific circumstances
– without an enemy in sight. Technical malfunctions, mistakes by
inexperienced pilots, bad judgement in taking off or landing, and
collisions – particularly among the sprawling bomber-fleets in the crowded
skies over East Anglia – caused terrible carnage. Even in the relatively
empty skies of America, pilots lost their lives in tragic training exercises.

DONALD F MUNDELL, USAAF

A lot of the training was done at night, and we lost quite a few planes on those night missions. They always burned when they crashed, and the fire could be seen from a long way at night, especially when you were in the air.

EMIL ANDERSON, USAAF

Plane crashes were always happening. Sometimes it would be months before a crash, and then a day would come and five or six planes would crash, either on landing or take-off. I can remember one day that a mock raid was held on Pearl Harbor, and during that attack 17 planes crashed. We just stood in groups and watched the disasters take place around us.

I saw a flight of five . . . flying in formation and in a blink of an eye three of them touched wingtips and went crashing into the bay. The sky was full of planes that day, diving, weaving and flying, and we watched as one came down on a dive-bomb run, and never pulled out, crashing into one of the hangers. Plane and hanger both burst into flames . . .

The craft in which these men flew and died were part of a rapid revolution in aircraft design. War, as it always does, proved a massive spur to invention, with designers and engineers working day and night to answer the problems of combat with new types of aeroplane or adjustments to existing ones.

In 1939 only the Soviet Union had an air force larger than Germany's, but the latter led the field in terms of technology and striking-power. With 4,300 aircraft, the Luftwaffe dwarfed the RAF, which had 1,911. German planes and pilots had gained highly useful combat experience in the Spanish Civil War. Men and machines were at a peak of prestige, confidence and readiness for a major conflict.

The Messerschmitt 109 was the most ubiquitous – because it was the most mass-produced – German fighter of the war. First built in 1935, it was ultimately to have a speed of 465mph and a ceiling of nearly 38,000ft. It was armed with three 30mm cannon (one of which fired through the nose-cone) and two 30mm machine guns. Between its debut and the end of the war it underwent, as did virtually all promising aircraft, constant modification to improve its speed, handling, armament and fuel supply. It therefore boasted a bewildering number of versions (D, E, F and so on). Naturally those who flew it were most fulsome in their praise of its later editions.

JOHANNES STEINHOFF, LUFTWAFFE

I flew the Messerschmitt 109 from the outbreak of war until the end. The Me109 was an excellent fighter, although during its long period of service it had many ups and downs. As the war drew on, it became increasingly unreliable, mainly due to the shortage of quality materials available. By the war's end, the average life of an Me109 was only 100 hours.

However, despite the plane's remarkable versatility it was not without a weakness.

HERMANN BUCHNER, LUFTWAFFE

My first unit, SG1, was equipped with the Me109E, with fuselage shackles for either a 300-litre fuel tank or one 250kg bomb or attachments for four 50kg bombs. We also carried splinter bombs. The Me109E was not an ideal aircraft for deep penetration ground attack missions due to its vulnerability to ground fire. A bullet in the cooling system would give the engine only three to five minutes before it seized.

JOSEPH HAIBÖCK, LUFTWAFFE

At the beginning of World War II the dominant fighter was the Messerschmitt BF 109E. I flew this aircraft throughout 1940, including the attack on England. At that time we had to acknowledge the outstanding flying characteristics of the British fighter aircraft, but we still felt superior on account of our weapons and our fuel-injected engines.

With continuous fine-tuning of design by engineers on the opposing sides, the technological edge passed alternately to the RAF and the Luftwaffe. Haiböck continued:

In 1941, we received the improved F series. Instead of the previous angular shape, this machine had smoothly flowing lines and, as a result, had greatly improved training ability. Then, in [that] summer, it became clear that [enemy] machines were improving greatly. The result was fierce aerial combat, for which we had to push our machines to the limit. As a result the air-frames became over-stressed. Without any damage from enemy fire, the wings became prone to coming off in flight and as a result of this we lost some very successful pilots. To land after a day's combat with the wings distorted out of shape was commonplace. The faults were later corrected by strengthening the air-frame, but our faith in the 109F was shattered . . .

Constant changes to the specification of the Me109 sometimes meant a compromise in quality.

ERNST WILHELM, LUFTWAFFE

I felt at the time, and still feel today, that the F variant was the best version we ever had. The G version, with all its modifications producing a bulge here and a bump there, was never quite the same thoroughbred. Although the engine had more power, it was also heavier and therefore, to accommodate this, the fuselage, engine mounts and landing gear had to be strengthened, substantially raising the overall weight. The result was increased speed but inferior manoeuvrability.

The Messerscmitt 109 had an able partner in the Focke-Wulf 190, which first appeared in 1941 and which also remained in use until the end of the war by undergoing numerous minor transformations. The stubby and angular FW-190 lacked the greyhound-sleekness of the Me109 but it was a more effective fighter and earned greater affection from pilots. The relationship between the two planes was similar to that between Hurricane and Spitfire – both were impressive, but friend and foe agreed that the former was distinctly outclassed by the latter.

Powered by a 14-cylinder supercharged engine and armed with two 7.9mm machine guns as well as four 20mm cannon, it had a maximum speed of 375mph. Its manoeuvrability was greater than the Spitfire's and it could climb faster, though it could not turn as tightly.

JOSEPH HAIBÖCK, LUFTWAFFE

... it gave us a much better chance against the numerically superior enemy. The one-piece wings could withstand a much greater wing loading, which gave us a smaller turning-radius. This advantage, and other improvements such as a wider undercarriage, meant that we readily accepted the teething problems ...

He concluded:

The Messerschmitt 109, at its inception, was a technical breakthrough in peace, but the FW-190 was a child of the war, proven at the front.

HERMANN BUCHNER, LUFTWAFFE

The FW-190 was more compact [than the 109] and, with its air-cooled engine, more resistant to ground-fire. Its wide undercarriage made it better suited to operating from makeshift airfields and it was well-armed and powerful.

ERICH RUDORFFER, LUFTWAFFE

... I could turn on a plate, the wings being white from condensation and to pull it out of a dive at 440mph was no problem. The Me109 wasn't strong enough to do that ...

JULIUS MEIMBURG, LUFTWAFFE

[The Focke-Wulf 190 was] a very modern aircraft which meant a reduced workload for the pilot. I think there was a total of thirteen functions, including the flaps, trim adjustment and start-up which were electronically controlled. In the 109 they were manual. [The 190] was infinitely superior, with the punishment the air-cooled engine could take. With the Me109 it was easy to receive a hit in the engine cooling system which left you at the mercy of the escorting fighters. I once saw a pilot return an FW-190 from England with two cylinder heads destroyed and his cockpit covered in oil, an incredible feat and a testimony to [the plane's] robustness ...

Although the plane was highly popular, it was not without its problems.

HERMANN BUCHNER, LUFTWAFFE

[It] had poor visibility on the ground and required an engine-change after only 40 to 50 flying hours, a six-hour job.

An aircraft that earned more distinctly mixed reviews was the Messerschmitt 110, a two-seat fighter-bomber that was much in evidence during the Battle of Britain. Too slow for a fighter and with too small a payload to make an effective bomber, many flyers considered it a death-trap. Developed in time to take part in the invasion of Poland, it performed well against a demoralized opposition whose tiny air force barely succeeded in getting off the ground, but this plane was a sitting target for RAF fighters, and suffered heavy losses. Nevertheless, it continued in service, often as a night-fighter.

HANS-JOACHIM JABS, LUFTWAFFE

I flew the Me110, both as a day and night fighter. The 110C and D models I flew in daylight proved inferior to the single-seat fighters over England, especially when compared to the Spitfire. The Me110C4 variant, for example, had a maximum speed of 350mph at 23,000ft, but lacked the manoeuvrability it needed. The D model [had] greater range but, by the summer of 1941, these had almost disappeared from the European theatre due to their unsuitability as day fighters against effective opposition.

PAUL ZORNER, LUFTWAFFE

Despite its unsuitability for daytime operations, it was the best night fighter available until . . . 1944. It had a good rate of climb, a three-and-a-half hour endurance, was sufficiently manoeuvrable, a good instrument flyer and was well armed. [In the G4 model] I got 42 victories, until it was destroyed by a daylight raid.

The Junkers 87 'Stuka' dive-bomber, which had been adapted from an American original, was an ideal weapon for accompanying fast-moving armies. Flying ahead of ground troops, it would drop its bomb-load with terrifying accuracy on fortified positions, tanks, communications systems and columns of troops – or refugees. It looked as malevolent as a vulture, and with the 'whistles' fitted in its landing gear its trademark became the hideous, siren-shriek it emitted when in a dive. Though it was successful in the war's early stages and continued to be used on the Eastern Front, its inadequacy swiftly became evident when it faced the RAF.

Though armed with cannon and a machine gun, the aircraft was so slow that it could be caught with ease by enemy fighters. Its two-man crew – a pilot and a backward-facing gunner – were enclosed in a raised glass cockpit that, though it afforded them an all-around view, left them completely exposed, and the plane was very lightly armoured. Hit from the side, or from above, they stood little chance of survival and, used briefly in the Battle of Britain, their losses were considerable. One RAF pilot famously described dog-fighting with Stukas as 'like shooting rats in a barrel'.

The Stuka was to have been replaced by 1939, though the war meant that it continued in service alongside its replacement, the Junkers 88. This was an extremely versatile aircraft, frequently used as a night fighter and fulfilling much the same position in the Luftwaffe as the (greatly superior) Mosquito held in the RAF. The Ju88 had good armament but again lacked the speed necessary for true effectiveness. Nevertheless, some pilots preferred it to the Dornier 217, which represented the next stage upward in terms of power, range and bomb-load.

PAUL ZORNER, LUFTWAFFE

I commenced my night-fighting career flying the Ju88, an aircraft that was sufficiently agile for this purpose, had a good rate of climb and an endurance of over three and a half hours. Its air-cooled radial engines were also relatively insensitive to enemy fire. I then flew the Dornier 217; a heavy aircraft designed purely as a bomber, with a consequently poor rate of climb and limited manoeuvrability. Its endurance of over five hours made it useful for missions over the sea, but it was not a popular aircraft. I personally thought it was a useless night-fighter.

In its development of a heavy bomber the Luftwaffe was severely hampered by the fact that the head of its Technical Development Department – the man with authority over aircraft design – was a single-minded proponent of the dive-bomber. Ernst Udet demanded that all German bombers have the capacity to dive, and this was a cause of major problems. It meant, for instance, that air-frames had to be reinforced and spoiled the balance of an aircraft. It also prevented the building, or use of, heavy bombers with a large payload, precisely the thing that the Allies were steadily introducing and that became such a crucial factor in turning the tide of war against Germany. Only after Udet's death in 1942 was the Luftwaffe free to move in this direction. By then the Battle of Britain was lost, the United States was involved and the initiative in the strategic air war was held by the Allies.

The Heinkel was the Luftwaffe's only attempt at a heavy bomber. Produced in two models, the 111 and the 117, and first seen in 1939, it too was made to conform to Udet's stipulation. Though it performed well on all fronts during the war, it compared badly with Allied aircraft and was somewhat dangerous to fly.

Germany developed a jet fighter at the end of 1944 and this briefly saw action in the war's final weeks. The Me262, sent up to tangle with the Allied bomber fleets over Berlin and other target areas, caused a good deal of havoc. With a speed of 540mph it was too fast for air-gunners to aim at or for pilots to avoid. Less than a hundred flew in combat, and the 262's arrival came too late to prevent the war's inevitable end. It represented a new era in air warfare and would undoubtedly have been decisive if used sooner or in greater numbers, even though it clearly suffered from teething problems.

HERMANN BUCHNER, LUFTWAFFE

The Me262 was 200kph faster than any Allied fighter, well armed (later with 24 RAM rockets) and suitable for instrument flying. For the time, it was technically outstanding, but we had no idea about the sound barrier and ejector seats. Also, the engines had to be changed after only 25 flying hours.

JOHANNES STEINHOFF, LUFTWAFFE

The Me262 jet fighter was the best wartime aircraft I flew. After the piston-engine machines, it was a new world. It had a self-starting unit, a small auxiliary power unit in front of the main engines, a nose-wheel brake and a working IFF system. But most remarkable of all was the armament. With four 30mm cannons, the firepower was devastating.

Its main drawback was the poor reliability of the power plants. If you touched the throttle above 20,000ft it would suffer compressor

stall and power from the engine would be lost. It also had an
endurance of only one hour 20 minutes.

In 1939, at the start of the war, the Royal Air Force possessed two
excellent but un-blooded fighters. The Hawker Hurricane, dating
from the same year as the Me109, and the Supermarine Spitfire, which
had been introduced a year later. Both were sleek, fast, well-armed
with machine guns or a cannon, and had an ability to turn and climb
that left enemy pilots in their wake. Both Allied and German airmen
regarded the Spitfire with awe – Luftwaffe pilots actually hated to
be shot down by anything less – and its technical performance was
without doubt superior. The Hurricane, however, earned a great deal
of affection for its sturdiness. Once again, the notion that an aircraft
could withstand the shocks and stresses of hard flying and enemy
bullets and still bring its pilot back was the factor that won the hearts
of those who flew the plane.

PETER TOWNSEND, RAF

The Hurricane had a more stable gun platform and a closer grouped
battery of four guns in each wing. It was also extremely robust and
easy to repair. In all, Hurricanes shot down more enemy aircraft
than did Spitfires during the Battle of Britain.

FRANK CAREY, RAF

Although other aircraft may have attracted more glamour and
boasted higher speeds, the Hurricane ploughed into every task that
it was given and still came back for more.

Built like the Forth Bridge, it could take enormous punishment
and yet get you home. On one occasion in the Battle of Britain, I had
my entire rudder and all but a tiny portion of one elevator blown off
together with a hole in the port wing that a man could have fallen
through . . . the Hurricane landed quite normally – even though it
needed a long rest.

BOB STANFORD-TUCK, RAF

... the Hurricane was a very sturdy old war-horse, with better
visibility for the pilot over the nose, and was admirably suited
for attacking bombers; indeed with crossfire from a large enemy
formation it was capable of standing very heavy damage.

This level of affection, however, is as nothing in comparison with the
devotion engendered by the Spitfire – one of the best-known planes ever
to have been manufactured. Pilots simply fell over themselves to shower
praise on it:

HUGH DUNDAS, RAF

Spitfires never let me down.

DANNY BROWNE, RCAF

The Spitfire IX was an incredible, immortal combat vehicle.

PADDY BARTHROPP, RAF

The aircraft was part of you and when frightened, either in testing
or in combat, I think one used to talk to one's Spitfire and I am
equally sure that it used to answer.

BOB HAYWARD, RCAF

Spitfire IX – the sweetheart of them all. You didn't fly it, you wore it
like a glove and waved it around!

Pilot's comments give some insight into the technical features of the plane
and the reasons these inspired such confidence.

JAMIE JAMESON, RAF

I preferred the Spitfire to the other fighter aeroplanes because it
had few vices. It was fast at all levels, very manoeuvrable and had
a very high rate of climb ...

BUD MALLOY, RCAF

The Spitfire IX was a delight to fly, was supremely responsive to the controls in all altitudes of flight and was a very stable gun platform . . .

ROD SMITH, RCAF

The Spitfire Mark IX was a far better fighting aeroplane than the earlier marks because it had the Rolls-Royce Merlin 60 Series engine, which had a two-stage supercharger. This device wrested the height advantage from the Germans and gave lasting command of the air to the Allies . . . They were marvellously nimble.

DENIS CROWLEY-MILLING, RAF

It felt part of you, it responded delightfully under all conditions, and most of all, it gave you ample warning of the high-speed stall in a turn in combat; and you knew that the Me 109 could not (or would not) turn inside you.

PETE BROTHERS, RAF

Whilst the Hurricane was ruggedly trustworthy at withstanding danger, my favourite was the Spitfire XIV, which exuded power and speed. Here was an aircraft in which it was a pleasure to be bounced from above and behind, for one could turn, open the throttle, climb steeply and take the diving enemy head-on . . .

Like its rivals on both sides, the Spitfire was subject to constant improvement as designers responded to both pilots' experiences and changes in enemy machines. The Spitfire, like the majority of fighters, had a vital blind spot: the pilot could not see directly astern. This was addressed with the fitting of a rear-view mirror. The related problem, of vulnerability to being machine-gunned from behind, was solved by the pilots themselves when they had steel plating bolted to the backs of their seats.

The Hurricane and Spitfire were joined by another versatile fighter – the

Hawker Typhoon. First seen in 1941, this came to maturity in the Northwest Europe Campaign. Formidably armed, it became the scourge of the retreating Germans when flying in support of tanks and infantry.

HUGH GODEFROY, RCAF

I flew the Typhoon from Normandy and found it a powerful and manoeuvrable brute, able to withstand punishment. With four 20mm cannon and two 500lb bombs or eight rockets, it was a very resilient fighter-bomber.

DENYS GILLAM, RAF

At first the Typhoon gave a lot of trouble – both the airframe and the engine – and we lost a lot of good pilots. However, once these [difficulties] were overcome it became a very tough and reliable machine and the very best gun platform. It carried bombs, rockets and cannon, and you could hold a steep dive longer than the Me109 or the FW-190. It could withstand high G-forces and its wide undercarriage was a great benefit on rough airfields.

It spawned an even more lethal cousin, the Tempest.

Much more famous as a fighter-bomber was the Mosquito – a two-engine, two-crew plane developed in 1940 but, again, achieving its greatest glory in the war's later stages. As with the Spitfire, those who flew it were unanimous in their praise.

DON BENNETT, RAF

Like so many flyers with a lot of hours logged on heavy bombers I found the Mosquito a beautiful aircraft . . . she was light, manoeuvrable, versatile and in just about every way a delight to fly.

ROY RALSTON, RAF

For the first time, [our bombers] could compete with German fighters as regards speed.

The Mosquito was very versatile; it could be used for a wide range of reconnaissance and bombing tasks by both day and night.

JACK V WATTS, RCAF

I flew Whitleys, Halifaxes and Mosquitos on bombing missions and the Mosquito was by far the best. For those of us in the Pathfinder Force it was the only aeroplane that could survive . . . the formidable German air-defences. Flying straight and level for ten minutes on our bombing run would have been certain death in any other bomber. We could deliver a bomb-load up to the 4,000lb blockbuster with pinpoint accuracy at ranges equal to any of the heavy bombers – and do the job in half the time.

IVOR BROOM, RAF

The Blenheim was obsolescent at the time, but the all-wooden and unarmed Mosquito was probably the most advanced and flexible aircraft of its time. Berlin and back in only four hours, and the Mosquito was then able to operate when poor weather forecasts prohibited lengthy flights by slower aircraft. At one period in 1944–45 it attacked Berlin for 25 nights running. At 25–28,000ft the German fighters couldn't touch it at night. A remarkable aircraft; a great credit to the designers and manufacturers.

CHRIS FOXLEY-NORRIS, RAF

. . . superb performance, handling and versatility . . . it could also absorb much punishment. Its manoeuvrability enabled us to attack almost inaccessible targets in Norwegian fjords and harbours and to evade both AA and fighter defences, and when necessary it could still return across the North Sea on one engine. It was incomparable.

Unlike the Luftwaffe, Britain had heavy bombers from the outbreak of war, but the lessons of combat quickly meant that slow or poorly-armed machines were discarded and that those types that performed well were adapted and improved. Thus the Whitley, the Ventura, the Blenheim and the Wellington, having served their purpose, were replaced by the Stirling, the Halifax and the Lancaster.

JAMES TAIT, RAF

Equipped with the slow Whitley IV, we had the only aircraft capable of reaching the long-range targets, and we bombed Berlin in 1940.

As technology progressed, the faults and flaws of the old bombers became evident; in this case the Wellington.

KEN BATCHELOR, RAF

It was not as fast as its four-engined successor; a round trip to Berlin took over eight hours. Moreover its operational ceiling was little more than half that later reached by Lancasters. This often meant flying in bad weather rather than over it, and it certainly attracted a great deal of flak . . .

The advent of the 'Lanc' in 1941 introduced a new era.

MICHAEL BEETHAM, RAF

I logged a few hours on other bomber types – Wellington, Stirling, Halifax, but they did not, as bombers, bear comparison with the Lancaster. One had complete confidence in it as a flying machine, being remarkably manoeuvrable for an aircraft of that size, having no vices and with the ever-comforting sound of the four Merlins.

JOHN BENISON, RAF

On one occasion our Lancaster had a shell burst in the starboard wing severing the main spar. With skilful piloting we survived the return . . . landing without further mishap at a stalling speed of just on 150mph. To be capable of this; or to carry a ten-ton bomb and land safely with the bomb still on board (as we did twice) is proof of a remarkable aircraft.

JOHN SEARBY, RAF

. . . fast, light on the controls and possessed [of] a good range, in addition to carrying a massive load of bombs . . . sweet to handle.

DANNY DANIEL, RCAF

As a bomb-aimer my prime consideration was how an aircraft performed in that role and there was none better than the Lancaster. It could carry huge loads, evidenced by the Grand Slam bombs which weighed 2,200lbs.

ROLAND HAMMERSLEY, RAF

I found the Lancaster the best-equipped aircraft for the wireless operator.

The US planes that began, from 1942 onwards, to fill the airfields of eastern England and the skies over Europe told a similar story of innovation and development. The American fighter was the Lockheed P-38, which was adept in its major role as bomber-escort, and the P-51 Mustang. The latter had in fact been commissioned by the RAF in 1940 and used since then, but the addition of a Merlin engine two years later improved an already outstanding performance.

GERALD BROWN, USAAF

I flew one tour in the P-38 and one in the P-51. I believe the 51 was a better combat aircraft against the German types. I never sweated fuel in the 51 and I always felt I could do anything the German could do . . .

The Mustang similarly attracted praise from the US and Canadian pilots, even though it was far from flawless.

RICHARD ROHMER, RCAF

... a solid, superbly-crafted piece of machinery, rugged and reliable. It was a poor dog-fighting aircraft because of its weight, but because of that weight and its streamlined contours and special wings it could outrun anything that flew.

The Mustang was the hero of the European air-war in its latter stages. It had a maximum speed of 475mph and a ceiling of 42,000ft. Its operational radius was 850 miles and thus it could accompany the bomber fleets all the way to their targets deep inside Germany, a factor without which the US could not have kept up its daylight campaign. Its six machine guns may have made it less powerful in a fight than the FW-190, but its speed, turn and climb were better. It really could 'outrun anything that flew'.

The Bombers that it accompanied were themselves great engineering achievements. The B-17 Flying Fortress and its sister-ship, the B-24 Liberator, appeared in such quantities (the Liberator was the war's most mass-produced aircraft) that they naturally dominated the bombing offensive. The B-17 had first been built in 1939. It could carry a bomb-load of up to 10,500lb a distance of nearly 2,000 miles and drop it with tremendous accuracy, and its top speed was just under 300mph.

MURRAY PEDEN, RCAF

My favourite combat bomber was the Fortress. It could climb, seemingly, forever; it was as sturdy under fire as the proverbial brick edifice, and it floated sufficiently on landing to forgive all but the crudest pilots. At altitude it did a corkscrew that would curl your hair. I owe my life to her quality – and love her still.

The B-24 was faster, but carried a smaller bomb-load and had a shorter range. Both planes had crews of ten or eleven, including a team of gunners. When planes flew in tight formation these could set up a maze of fire that few enemy fighters would dare to approach. Their opponents were initially able to exploit a weak point in their armament.

ALFRED GRISLAWSKI, LUFTWAFFE

In fighting in the 'Defence of the Reich', the attacks on the enemy bombers were the most frightening, with our methods of frontal attack requiring particularly strong nerves. We used this method to attack the B-17 'Fortress' bombers, since this was their weakest area (although in later versions, the Americans countered this by installing a forward firing turret beneath the nose). I especially remember the Schweinfurt raids where huge formations of bombers flew in without fighter escort. The defensive fire that they could produce was enormous and the large amounts of tracer visibly flying through the air as we went in to attack was very demoralizing. We suffered enormous casualties, although, from a defenders point of view, the operations were a success. I myself shot down two four-engined bombers during the first raid. I was then hit myself, but managed to nurse my aircraft back to our airfield at Erbenheim where I was able to land with my engine stopped.

On the Eastern Front the Germans faced some of the same enemy machines, for Britain and America sent aircraft to their Soviet ally, and in the latter part of the war some US bomber crews flew from Russian airfields. The Soviet Air Force badly needed help as it entered the conflict, for the Luftwaffe had targeted its airfields and aircraft with such accuracy that in the first nine hours of the invasion more than 1,200 planes were destroyed, and after a week's fighting less than 10 per cent of Soviet frontline air strength remained. Nevertheless both Russian aircraft design and the massive efforts of Soviet industry to keep up production were highly impressive.

The basic fighter was the 'Yak', named after its designer, AS Yakovlev. This became available at the precise time – June 1941 – that the Russian war started. It was in use throughout, and appeared in no less than 11 versions. The Yak-1 could reach a speed of over 370mph, had a ceiling of 32,000ft and a range of about 580 miles. Steady improvements meant that in its final form, the Yak-9P, it could fly at 416mph and operate at over

34,000ft to a range of 1,367 miles. Yaks were armed with a nose-mounted cannon, two machine guns and the option of bombs or rockets. Though initially inferior to German fighters, the Yak's steady improvement made the Luftwaffe increasingly cautious, and by the middle of the war they saw it as an equal.

The most effective Soviet bomber was the Petlyakov. Starting life in 1939 as a fighter, it underwent the inevitable modifications common to successful aircraft, and saw five different versions. These included the addition of dive-brakes and the fitting of bomb bays in the engine nacelles. The plane had a maximum speed of between 336 and 408mph, depending on the version. It could operate, ultimately, at a height of more than 36,000ft and to a distance of nearly 750 miles, it had a crew of three and was armed with four machine guns. It could carry 2,200lb of bombs. Considerably better than the German Stuka, this plane was the equivalent of the Ju88, and was a worthy counterpart of the Mosquito.

In the Pacific, the Zero – the Mitsubishi A6M – was by far the most well-known aircraft. A carrier-launched naval fighter, it easily outclassed – in quality or quantity – anything available to its American, British or Dutch opponents in the war's opening stages, and came to symbolize the unstoppability of the Japanese war machine. It was fast, with an ultimate top speed of 360mph, and could reach almost 40,000ft. Fitted with a drop-tank for long-range flying it could go almost 2,000 miles and could deliver two 132lb bombs. Highly manoeuvrable, it was a formidable enemy in a dogfight and its weaponry – two cannon, two machine guns and two bombs – gave it the versatility to undertake bombing missions, reconnaissance and support of ground forces as well as aerial combat, though its weakness was a tendency to catch fire easily. Flown by the Kamikaze units, it participated in Japan's final, desperate defensive air battle.

The Zero's nemesis was a pair of snub-nosed American fighters, the Gruman Wildcat and its sister, the Hellcat. Both were extremely durable, cheap to produce and, as a result, were manufactured in enormous numbers. As short, folded-wing planes (the bigger of the two, the Hellcat, had a wingspan of just over 42ft) they could fly from the smallest escort carriers. The Wildcat, built to a pre-war design used by the Royal Navy, could fly at up to 332mph, climb to 35,000ft and travel 900 miles. It carried no cannon but boasted up to eight machine guns, six in the wings and two in the fuselage, and had two 250lb bombs.

The Hellcat, built in 1942, was in every way an improvement. Its top speed was 376mph, its operational ceiling 37,500ft, and its range just over 1,000 miles. It too had six machine guns but it also had six rockets as well as a bomb-load of 2,000lbs. These aircraft, more than any others, won the air war against Japan.

2

BATTLE OF BRITAIN

The Battle of Britain was Hitler's first defeat. By June 1940 German armies had vanquished Poland and France and overrun the Netherlands, Belgium, Denmark and Norway. Many Germans assumed the war was over. Britain, the only remaining adversary, had no reason to continue fighting and, following her army's humiliating exit from Dunkirk, seemed incapable of doing so. Hitler expected her government to accept the position and sue for peace.

Yet it soon became apparent that this would not happen. Britain remained defiant and was clearly preparing for a long war. The German leader made 'a last appeal to reason' through a speech aimed at the British public. It backfired. His enemy was as implacably hostile and determined as before.

Invasion of England seemed the only alternative, and Hitler issued a directive ordering the Luftwaffe to create the necessary conditions for a seaborne landing. Goering saw this as involving three phases: firstly, the RAF must be driven from the skies of southern England, giving Germany complete air superiority. Secondly, the Channel must be cleared of the Royal Navy and minefields sown either side of the invasion route to forestall interference. Thirdly, the attacking force itself, carried in a fleet of commandeered river-barges, would cross from France. The Führer, assured by Goering that this could be achieved fully and swiftly, announced that he expected to receive Britain's surrender on 15 August.

The Battle of Britain began on 10 July 1940 and lasted until mid-September, though it merged with the 'Blitz' which continued into the following year. The Luftwaffe was unable to complete even the first phase of the operation before autumn weather in the Channel caused postponement of the invasion. By the following summer German efforts were concentrated on the other side of Europe and Operation Sea Lion had been indefinitely delayed.

Germany had expected to win. Her air force heavily outnumbered Britain's (the Luftwaffe had almost 2,800 front line aircraft; the RAF had 700). Her pilots had more combat experience than their adversaries, and the capture of airfields in northern France and Belgium had brought the whole of south-east England within range of her fighters and bombers.

But the RAF had already proved the toughest opponent the Luftwaffe had faced. British pilots too had gained experience, in France, where they had taken a heavy toll of German aircraft. Their Hurricanes and Spitfires could outmanoeuvre the lumbering bombers, which had neither the speed nor the protection to survive sustained attack. The Spitfire was fully the equal of the German Me109, but had a significant advantage: over England, a 109 was operating at the extent of its range. The journey to London left only enough fuel to fly escort – or fight – for ten minutes before turning for home. Lack of fuel could mean ditching in the Channel, a fate that befell most pilots at least once.

A British flyer, shot down over friendly territory, could be back in the air within hours. Any German who escaped a burning aircraft knew he was out of the war entirely, and this had an important effect on morale, as did the amateurish but autocratic leadership of Goering.

Most significantly, Britain possessed a trump card which her opponents had failed to appreciate. British radar was much more advanced and effective than its German counterpart. A chain of radar stations, along the coast, could identify the range, altitude and direction of approaching aircraft and enable the RAF to intercept them with pinpoint accuracy.

Nevertheless the struggle was intense. Pursuing their first objective, the Luftwaffe hit the RAF stations of south-east England in an unremitting series of attacks. The pounding went on day after day until Britain's air defences were close to collapse. Machines were being lost more quickly than they could be replaced; crews were exhausted from flying continuous sorties. For all their courage, the RAF could not have stood much more.

What saved them – and Britain – was a German mistake. Hitler had forbidden the Luftwaffe, for the moment, to attack London. He believed the destruction of the capital would harden British resolve. The decision regarding such a move was his alone to make.

On 24 August, however, it was made for him. That night two aircraft, lost in the darkness over England, released their bombs over east London. This was seen as opening a new phase of the war, and Churchill retaliated by ordering a raid on Berlin the following night. The resulting damage was slight, but provoked Hitler to such a fury that he demanded a massive campaign against British cities. The Luftwaffe's abrupt change of targets, though tragic for the civilian population, allowed the RAF to repair airfields, train more pilots and replace lost aircraft.

German fliers believed that the RAF was reduced to its last few planes, yet every wave of bombers was met by swarms of British fighters. They could not imagine where these men and machines were coming from.

During the summer and autumn British aircraft production grew to outstrip both its losses and its opponents (1,900 fighters, against the Germans' 775). To offset delays caused by the bombing of factories, production of parts was spread throughout the country. To provide pilots, almost every qualified RAF flyer was retrained for fighters, while the glamour of the Service ensured a continuing supply of recruits. Training was often rushed, and many inexperienced pilots died, but they kept the RAF in the air for long enough to outlast the Luftwaffe offensive.

This ended, eventually, following the German attack on Russia. Hitler considered the British to be virtually beaten and decided that they could be finished off later. Fortunately for civilisation, it was a fatal miscalculation.

* * *

For many pilots the air war began gradually as the anticipated hordes of bombers failed to materialize. However, some were in at the very beginning:

DIETER HRABAK, LUFTWAFFE

When the war started, I was Squadron Commander in the rank
of Oberleutnant in I./JG 76, flying escort missions and fighter
sweeps from an emergency airfield in Upper Silesia. During
the Polish campaign, at the outset of the war, I only once met
enemy aircraft in the sky. This was on 3 September 1939, when I
attacked a flight of Polish light bombers, however before I started
shooting, my engine was hit by [one of their] rear gunners. I belly-
landed my aircraft between the lines and hid in a nearby forest
until I was picked up by an advancing German armoured unit.
My method of attack had been naïve and had taught me a number
of valuable lessons: firstly, think before attacking, familiarize
yourself with the relevant enemy aircraft types, carry a hand
weapon and finally wear your uniform (I had worn a sports shirt)
in case of capture.

At the beginning of the French campaign, my unit flew combat
patrols above our fast-moving tank divisions, operating from an
emergency airstrip near Trier. Flying four or five missions a day,
I achieved my first aerial victory on 13 May 1940, over a French
Potez 63, a twin-engine reconnaissance aircraft.

SANDY JOHNSTONE, RAF

Together with pilots of 603 (City of Edinburgh) Squadron, I took part
in the first historical fighter engagement over the United Kingdom
on 16 October 1939, when German bombers attacked naval units
moored near the Forth Bridge. My first victory was at night when
I attacked a Heinkel bomber caught in the searchlights – it crashed
into the sea and the crew were taken prisoner.

People went about their everyday business with little idea of
what was taking place high in the sky. Usually all they saw was the
ever-changing patterns of our white vapour trails, but sometimes
they would see us as a number of tiny specks scintillating like
diamonds in the strong sunlight of those cloudless days.

More commonly, on the British side at least, the first taste of action came only after months of routine, but the tension built up as the summer of 1940 approached:

PETER TOWNSEND, RAF

Soon after the outbreak of war, 43 Squadron was moved to Acklington to perform convoy patrol duties, and on 3 February 1940, leading 'B' Flight, we shot down an He111, the first German to crash on English soil since World War I. Later that month I claimed my first solo victory, an He111 which I shot down at 20,000ft. Both his wings were shorn off in his 'death dive'.

I brought down another He111 in April, and was promoted to lead 85 Fighter Squadron in May 1940. I had further combats against Dornier aircraft during the spring and by mid-summer the Squadron was becoming more and more intensively engaged with enemy aircraft. During the height of the Battle of Britain I led 85 Squadron's Hurricanes against the mass Luftwaffe attacks over the Thames estuary. On 18 August, I claimed an Me110 and two Me109s. The next two weeks saw the fiercest fighting – of 20 pilots in 85 Squadron, 14 were shot down (two of them twice), some killed, some wounded.

FRANK CAREY, RAF

In early May 1940, the air over northern France and Belgium fairly teemed with German aircraft, mostly without fighter escort. With this backing my luckiest sorties began promisingly enough when I saw a Heinkel 111 with one engine feathered. A short burst at the working elastic abruptly terminated its flight. Minutes later a great gaggle of some 60-odd Ju87 Stukas hove into view. The Stuka had the rather obliging habit of bursting into flames almost as soon as one opened fire. Two of these performed predictably and hit the ground and two others were following suit on their away down when I saw a beautiful bright silver Do17 float across my bows. Giving it the remainder of my ammunition in one long burst, it slewed violently with much smoke pouring out, but being very short of fuel I turned hurriedly for base. The conspicuous Do17 was confirmed by a fellow pilot who saw it crash.

As the conflict reached a pitch of intensity, pilots became all too familiar with both the adrenalin-rush of combat and the instantaneous, tragic loss of friends:

BOB STANFORD-TUCK, RAF

At 1045 on 23 May 1940, No 92 (F) Squadron took off from Hornchurch, led by Squadron Leader Roger Bushell, and headed for a patrol line of Dunkirk, Calais, Boulogne. At 1145 hours a large number of Me109s dropped on us in a steep diving attack. Pat Learmond's Spitfire immediately went down in a ball of flame – sadly 92 Squadron's first casualty of the war. As the Me109s pulled up, using full throttle, I was able to get in behind one which had turned for home. Skimming the top of some cloud I closed on him knowing that he hadn't seen me. After some tense moments I had him centrally in my gun sight. At 300 yards I pushed the firing button and the Me109 performed a violent upward manoeuvre followed by three flick-rolls, went over on its back into a vertical dive, shedding debris.

At near maximum speed I followed him through a thin layer of cloud at 16,000ft, but he made no attempt to pull out and hit the deck with an almighty explosion just outside St Omer. This was my first victory.

Later that day the Squadron was again in heavy combat over Dunkirk, and we lost our Squadron Commander, John Gillies, Paddy Green and Sergeant Klipsch. I shot down two twin-engine Me110s during the dogfight, bringing my tally to three on my first day in combat.

While much of the air war was naturally concentrated on western Europe and the Channel, the RAF was obliged to go wherever the enemy were operating. Some found themselves facing the Germans in a very unfamiliar environment.

JAMIE JAMESON, RAF

On 28 May 1940, I was told that German transport aeroplanes were unloading troops in a fjord south of Narvik. Eventually we spied two enormous six-engine flying boats hidden in a small cove and protected by high cliffs on three sides of the cove. To attack the boats we had to dive steeply down the side of one cliff, firing as we went, and then had to make a steep turn along the fjord to avoid the cliff on the other side. When we left, the flying boats were blazing and sinking.

After a few weeks we were ordered to evacuate Norway and our Commanding Officer, 'Bing' Cross, decided that rather than burn our precious Hurricanes we should try and land on *Glorious* – the first time modern fighters had attempted to land on an aircraft carrier. I led the first section of three Hurricanes and after some anxious moments we got down safely. The following day Bing brought the remaining seven Hurricanes and they, too all got down all right. The next day, 8 June 1940, we were intercepted and shelled by two German battleships, *Scharnhorst* and *Gneisenau*.

I made my way to the quarter deck and saw the two cruisers six or seven miles astern and firing at the doomed *Glorious*, whose guns did not have the range to fire back. Eventually the 'Abandon Ship' order was passed and someone said the bridge had received a direct hit and that the captain was dead.

I was the last to leave the ship alive. I swam about a mile to the nearest raft and was delighted to see Bing Cross already there. At 1800 that evening we had 29 on the Carley float. We were well inside the Arctic Circle and after about four hours the first man died of exposure. The following morning only ten of us were

left alive. We spent three nights on the raft, when a Norwegian
fishing boat picked up seven survivors, but a further man died
in the boat and another on arrival in the Faroes. There were only
five survivors.

The majority of fighter pilots were in action nearer home. As the British
Army was evacuated from France, their support was vital in minimizing
the havoc wrought by the Luftwaffe.

DAVID SCOTT-MALDEN, RAF

The squadrons were dropping supplies on the besieged garrisons
of Calais and Boulogne, and were rapidly running out of pilots. The
outlook was bleak . . .

PADDY BARTHROPP, RAF

We flew to Calais in a Lysander to drop supplies for the beleaguered
British troops. We were fired at from the ground, and since Marcus
had a number one gun stoppage, or something like that, he tore the
gun from the mounting and threw it at the enemy troops below. On
our return we found that our mission was in vain because our troops
had surrendered the day before.

Another flyer recalled the moment at which, during those hectic weeks,
two giants of the air war were first formally introduced:

ALAN DEERE, RAF

It has officially been recognized that I was the first Spitfire to
engage in a dogfight with a Messerschmitt 109 fighter. Of all my
combats this one remains most clear in my memory, not because
it was the most successful or exciting but because it was the first
in which I first became aware of the greatness of the Spitfire. It
took place near Calais on the morning of 23 May during the
Dunkirk evacuation.

On arrival over Calais with my number two, Johnnie Allen, we ran into some 109s, combat being immediately joined. I destroyed one of these 109s almost at first contact through a combination of good luck, in that he unknowingly crossed in front of me, allowing my guns to bear with little skill on my part, and the pilot's subsequent poor reaction under fire. However, it is not this particular combat which proved the worth of the Spitfire but an inconclusive one which followed almost immediately as a fellow German tried to reap his revenge for his comrade.

At the precise moment of victory number one, a warning shout over the radio transmitter from Johnnie alerted me to the presence of an Me109 which was clearly manoeuvring to get on my tail. It was then I first became aware of the Spitfire's superior turning circle for I was able, after a bit of sparring, to get in behind the 109 though not in firing range. Now the fun started and thus the scene was set for the first sustained dogfight between a Spitfire and a Messerschmitt. When the Hun pilot realized he could be out-turned he reverted to less conventional and more violent manoeuvres. One moment I was watching his tail and the next I was presented with a clear view of the 109's pale blue underbelly. Desperate attempts followed to shake me off, but I managed to stick with him. At no time, however, could I bring my guns to bear although I did from time to time give him a burst, but with no apparent effect for I was never really in range. He, I am sure, was desperate but then so too was I because I was getting short of fuel and I had exhausted my ammunition. I could so easily become the hunted, but the adrenalin of battle was by now flowing freely and the urge to prove that anything he could do in his 109 could be matched in my Spitfire was paramount in my thoughts. And so we remained locked for a little longer when, sanity at last restored, I chose an advantageous moment to break off and head for home with all speed.

In my report of this combat I stated categorically that the Spitfire could out-fly, except in the dive, and outfight the Messerschmitt. Little credence was given to this assertion by the pundits who were still beguiled by the Me109's success against the Hurricanes in France and, of course having due regard to this New Zealander's inexperience. In a few short weeks, the Battle of Britain was to prove me right.

Hard on the heels of the retreating British troops came the air assault on southern England and the months of frantic struggle that became known to history as the Battle of Britain. The lives of those in front-line squadrons became an exhausting sequence of tense boredom and excitement – long hours of restive waiting punctuated by moments of challenge, exhilaration, horror, pain – and even humour.

HUGH DUNDAS, RAF

22 August 1940, RAF Kenley – 616 Squadron had been released at about 1700, but was recalled to readiness an hour later. Winston Churchill was visiting the station, unexpectedly, and was talking to 616 Squadron when it was scrambled – a put-up job, I imagined.

Twenty minutes later at 12,000ft over Dover, two violent explosions put my Spitfire out of action. It immediately started to spin and the cockpit canopy jammed. I eventually got out at about 800ft, just in time to use my parachute.

I had learned, the hard way, about the proverbial Hun in the sun, and never forgot the lesson.

PETER TOWNSEND, RAF

31 August 1940, Croydon – Kenley Controller: 'Please come to readiness immediately.' There was a mad rush by pilots in old cars, motorbikes and bicycles to dispersal. I ordered pilots into cockpits, and to start-up, and I called controller: 'Can we go? I don't want to be bombed on the ground.' Controller: 'No hurry, old boy.' Looked round at my squadron, 12 Hurricanes, noses tilted skywards, propellers turning and glinting in the sun, all raring to go.

A moment later, controller: 'Off you go – and hurry!' As my

undercarriage raised, the engine cut, spluttered, then recovered
– caused by the blast from bombs exploding just behind, where the
rest of my squadron somehow got airborne, obscured by smoke.
Above were Dorniers, escorted by Me110s and Me109s. I climbed
at full boost with hood open, (better to watch out for Me109s) and
reached the Me110s first. As I attacked, a shower of Me109s fell
upon me spraying streams of tracer from behind. A 109 turned
in front, I hit him and he streamed vapour and slowed up. Then
another, I hit him too and he rolled over and, streaming vapour,
dived. A third just below – I could easily see the pilot, but while
manoeuvring to shoot, a Me110 came at me, firing head-on. My
Hurricane was badly hit in the windscreen and self-sealing centre
tank but mercifully there was no fire. I was hit in the foot by a
20mm explosive shell, and momentarily lost control in a dive. I
baled out low down over woods, just missing some large oaks, and
tumbling among fir saplings. After convincing the Home Guard and
a policeman of my nationality, we all adjourned to the Royal Oak,
Hawkhurst for drinks all round and a wonderfully friendly little
crowd to wave me off to hospital.

A dogfight, though it demanded intense skill and concentration, would
commonly be over in a matter of minutes, or even seconds:

DENIS CROWLEY-MILLING, RAF

On 31 August 1940, 242 Squadron led by Douglas Bader intercepted
a formation of Dornier and Heinkels escorted by Me110s northeast of London near North Weald, and estimated to be over one
hundred aircraft in all. It was an eerie sight, and the first time we
had seen such a mass of enemy aircraft in one piece of sky – the
Me110s on the flanks and others behind stepped up well above us
as we approached their left flank. However, almost before we could
take it all in, Douglas dived the Squadron, sections in fairly close
formation, right into the centre causing the 110s on the flank to

turn towards us, but too late to engage us [before we were]
in against the bombers. The Squadron claimed 12 aircraft
destroyed in all . . .

DAL RUSSEL, RCAF

In early September 1940, I was flying Blue 3 when we sighted
enemy bombers and as we attacked we were harried by Me109s
from starboard and above; as I broke away I came up under
three 109s flying in line astern. I gave the last 109 a three-second
burst at about 70 yards, noting strikes on his belly and he soon
baled out. His leader and number two took violent evasive action
and I eventually lost them. Shortly afterwards I climbed to attack
a gaggle of Me110s and fired from above and behind at the
last fighter. I gave him about a ten-second burst which set his
starboard engine on fire and he rolled over, one parachute
came out and he crashed just south of Biggin Hill. Still above
the Me110s, I attacked another and saw strikes on his cockpit
before my ammunition ran out. The Me110 went into a lazy
spiral and crashed several miles from the first, somewhere in
the Maidstone area.

PETE BROTHERS, RAF

On 15 September 1940, I was leading eight Hurricanes of 257
Squadron over London when I sighted a formation of Dorniers
in five lines of five aircraft abreast, all at 18,000ft, with escorting
yellow-nosed Me109s at 23,000ft.

I led a quarter attack developing into astern and fired a three-
second burst at 250 yards, closing, at the middle backline Do17.
The plane's port engine and rear fuselage caught fire and as I
followed it down the pilot baled out. The other backline bombers
focused heavy fire on me but caused only minor damage. On
breaking away, I saw and attacked a lone Do215, which crashed
two miles from Sevenoaks.

BOBBY OXSPRING, RAF

On 18 September 1940, flying Spitfire MkIIs with 66 Squadron, on
patrol at 30,000ft over Dover, we sighted a flight of Me109s crossing
our track. I attacked the rearmost 109, which was heading for cover
in thick cirrus cloud and managed to get in two short bursts of
fire. The enemy aircraft immediately burst into flames. The pilot
baled out, parachuting into the Channel two miles off Folkestone,
and was made POW. Records established the pilot as Leutnant
Erich Bodendeik of JG53 Ace of Spades group, with whom I now
correspond.

DENYS GILLAM, RAF

I left 616 Squadron and joined 312 (Czech) Squadron at Speke on
8 October 1940. As I was taking off in my Hurricane I saw a Ju88
crossing the boundary of the airfield and I closed to 100 yards,
opened fire and saw many strikes on the enemy bomber, which
landed close to the airfield, so I completed the circuit and landed.
I believe this was the fastest confirmed victory, the time from take-
off to landing being about eight minutes.

DAVID SCOTT-MALDEN, RAF

The aerial combat which remains vividly in my mind was over
Kent on 12 October 1940 soon after joining No 603 Squadron. The
Squadron was depleted by losses and eight aircraft were directed
into a large 'gaggle' of Me109s. The Squadron split up individually
and passed head-on through the enemy formation. There was a
sense of shock, as a distant series of silhouettes suddenly became
rough metal with grey-green paint and yellow noses, passing
head-on on each side. At the far end I had a few minutes'
dogfight with the last 109, scoring hits which produced a trail of
black smoke. Then we were alone at 20,000ft, the German gliding
down with an engine which coughed and barely turned over, I with
no ammunition and very little petrol. He glided hopefully towards

the Channel; I looked for an airfield before the last of my petrol ran out. Strangely I felt inclined to wave to him as he left. But then, I was only 20 years old.

SANDY JOHNSTONE, RAF

Whilst in the midst of a break at lunchtime, 602 Squadron was scrambled to deal with an enemy raid approaching the Isle of Wight at 15,000ft. In spite of the short warning, we made the interception before the Bandits reached the south coast. They consisted of some 50 plus Ju88s and Do17s, with a sizeable covering escort of Me109s and 110s.

I immediately despatched Findlay Boyd to take 'B' Flight against the escorts whilst I led 'A' Flight into the bomber formations. A free-for-all soon developed and I managed to down a 110 by blowing its tail unit clean off. I saw the pilot baling out of his spinning aircraft.

As I pulled up to rejoin the fray, an Me109 got on my tail, firing tracer but, in my anxiety to climb away from him, I accidentally stalled my aircraft and almost flipped over on top of my adversary. Indeed I was presented with such a point-blank target that even I could not fail to hit it, thus notching up my second confirmed victim in the one action.

The Squadron tally that day amounted to 13 enemy aircraft destroyed and four probably destroyed, without loss.

Luftwaffe pilots, guessing that their enemy must have some sort of secret weapon, were astonished at the accuracy of RAF strikes on their aircraft formations:

HANS-EBERHARD BOB, LUFTWAFFE

In cases of [escorting] a particularly large German bomber formation we flew between two cloud layers. For that reason we felt relatively safe because there was close cloud cover above and beneath us. To our surprise we were suddenly attacked by a large Spitfire formation exactly [in our] rear. At first it was incomprehensible how this formation could reach us in the rear without any sight[ing by us] in such a good attack position. Later we learned that the British were at that time already in possession of a kind of radar that could [guide them] exactly in height and direction.

Another thing that astonished the attackers was the seemingly inexhaustible supply of pilots. Surely the Allies could not produce qualified flyers so quickly? The explanation was only discovered at a later date.

JOHANNES STEINHOFF, LUFTWAFFE

The English had ingeniously found a way to defend their island. Every pilot, except a small group of night flyers and bomber pilots who were the nucleus of the coming night bomber fleet, was retrained as a fighter pilot. It made no difference if he was a liaison plane pilot, a bomber or fighter-bomber pilot, he was retrained. Industry was instructed to concentrate on fighters. And in this way it was possible to seal the gap – and more! In one stroke, the lost air superiority was regained, and henceforth we did not own the airspace from Calais to London.

With intense determination on both sides, fighting was fierce and losses were constant.

JULIUS MEIMBERG, LUFTWAFFE

Late in the afternoon of 28 November 1940, we took off for southern England from Beaumont le Roger for our second mission of the day. Climbing towards the Isle of Wight in bright sunshine, I was leading the 4th Staffel and directly ahead of us was the Staff Schwarm of JG2 Richthofen led by our Kommodore, Major Helmut Wick, at that time the leading fighter pilot in the Luftwaffe. With him were his wingman Oberleutnant Rudi Pflanz, Oberleutnant Leie and Oberfeldwebel Rudorffer. At about 23,000ft, we were almost above the Isle of Wight when we spotted vapour trails caused by Spitfires above us at a much greater height.

Major Wick led his Staff Schwarm towards them at full throttle, with the result that the Schwarm aircraft pulled apart from each other. Climbing with my Staffel to one side, we were soon drawn into the main battle and the Staffel separated. A single Spitfire turned in front of me and disappeared behind my engine cowling as I fired off my weapons. Apparently undamaged, the aircraft went into a spin and I followed it down, expecting the aircraft to pull out at any time, but it never did. The red glow in the cockpit indicated a possible oxygen tank hit.

When we landed, Rudi Pflanz reported that Major Wick had shot down a Spitfire, was then in turn shot down by a second, which in turn had been shot down by Pflanz. We were all told that no one had seen what had happened to Wick's aircraft, which left us hoping for the safety of our Kommodore. We returned later next day, and again the following day, but there was no sign of him. What we hadn't been told was that Rudorffer had witnessed him go down, a large bullet-hole passing through the starboard wing trailing edge, straight through the cockpit and engine block. He felt that Wick was already dead as his aircraft corkscrewed downwards, finally plunging into the sea. After the war, I learned that his conqueror had been Flight Lieutenant John Dundas DFC, himself only seconds later shot down by Pflanz and killed.

Their list of 'kills' was understandably an important measure of status among pilots, and a light-hearted approach to destroying the enemy – as if the battle were a school inter-house competition – boosted morale and helped offset the deadly seriousness of the situation.

HM STEPHEN, RAF

At the end of November 1940, the Station scoreboard at Biggin Hill was nearing the 600 mark, and naturally every pilot on the Station was hoping that he would shoot down the 600th victim, especially as most people on the airfield had subscribed to a handsome prize for the lucky pilot. However, on 1 November, before 0800 hours the Operations Staff rang through to advise that a small convoy in the Channel was being attacked by German fighter-bombers. Flight Lieutenant Mungo-Park, a great fighter pilot and leader, and I took off and aided by some clever controlling from the ground we saw a large German fighter wing returning to France at very high altitude. With skillful stalking we selected a 109 on the edge of one of the outside formations flying at the then great height of 35,000ft. I opened fire with a short burst from the starboard quarter. Then Mungo-Park went in and when I made my second attack I saw pieces flying off the 109, which eventually crash-landed inland from Dungeness.

The German perspective on events was given by one Luftwaffe pilot, who flew bomber escorts in a 109, and remembered the disadvantages of meeting the enemy so far from home:

HEINZ LANGE, LUFTWAFFE

In total I flew 76 sorties across the Channel, of which 32 were to London and 13 were carrying bombs. Most of our trips were tied up accompanying bombers and we were frustrated when the British fighters avoided contact with us, concentrating on the bombers. As a result, I had only 20 direct contacts and could not chalk up any aerial victories. However, I took comfort in the fact that many fine pilots were affected in the same way and, more importantly, I never lost a wingman or damaged an Me109 in a landing incident.

I still have vivid memories of my many sorties over England in the summer and autumn of 1940 and early 1941. It was extremely

tough and, in an effort to gain the best performance from our
aircraft, we used to polish them which would give an extra
5kmh or so. However, this advantage was immediately cancelled
if we carried any ancillaries. We would have benefited from
auxiliary fuel tanks to increase our range, but we never got them.
The Me110s carried extra tanks, but they weren't jettisonable,
so they were highly explosive during air battles, particularly
along Flak Street towards London. To add to this hazard were
barrage balloons at altitudes up to 4,500ft and the British radar
prevented us from being able to carry out surprise attacks.
The Spitfires were always above us, waiting, initially flying in
tight groups of three Vics deep. We, in turn, were not able to
communicate with the bombers we were trying to protect – a
disastrous shortcoming.

While Spitfires may have been above the bombers, they had problems of
their own:

PETER TOWNSEND, RAF

Invariably we had height disadvantage and we were frequently
jumped by Me109s when attacking bombers. Added to that their
technique – terrifying for both sides – was to fly straight at the
enemy aircraft: we used a hair-raising head-on attack to take out
leading bombers, which left the rest confused with nobody to follow!

Another German fighter pilot's account mentions one of these face-offs:

EDUARD NEUMANN, LUFTWAFFE

We were flying bomber escort at about 14,500ft, at the very slow
speed of our charges. Suddenly, a British fighter flew through us at
high speed, with [Adjutant] Bode in his flight path, and gave a short
burst before diving away below. No one had seen him approaching.
Bode started to lose engine coolant and the fate of this popular man

was sealed. We later discovered that he had emergency landed in England and been captured.

On another mission near London in September 1940 I watched British fighters climb to intercept our bombers, but before I could attack them another British unit flew directly at us and a real nose-to-nose shooting match developed. Then, suddenly, I felt a bang on the right wing, which made the aircraft shudder and immediately had to cut back the speed and lose height. England was covered in low cloud everywhere, so I was silhouetted as I descended. Unable to dive at speed, minutes felt like hours and the hole in my wing looked enormous.

Eventually reaching cloud cover, I nursed my crippled fighter eastwards. After landing safely in France, I inspected the damage and discovered that there had been an explosion in my 20mm cannon magazine, which had left a hole underneath so large that it would have taken both arms to encircle it. Had this happened to the upper wing surface, it is doubtful whether the aircraft would have continued to fly.

Yet with a sizeable numerical advantage, the waves of bombers kept on coming. One pilot of a Ju88 wrote a diary in which he described the experience of flying a raid over London during the autumn of 1940.

PETER STAHL, LUFTWAFFE

Over Lille is our agreed meeting point with units from other Geschwader. Eventually there is an assembly of at least 200 bombers that gathers into some order and sets course for London. Soon afterwards we are joined by an escort of Bf-109s and Bf-110s. The cloud cover beneath us gradually breaks up so that Hans can navigate according to his map.

Flying as an individual in a formation made up of three bombers, two fighters and one Bf Geschwader gives one a feeling of security. Wherever one looks are our aircraft, all around, a marvellous sight.

Among ourselves we estimate that the total bomb load destined to fall on London soon afterwards amounts to at least 200,000kg. And this has been going on for some days already. Poor London!

While crossing the Channel our formations sort themselves out. The fighters begin to fly a zigzag course alongside, above and underneath us. The British Isles greet us with quite accurate AA salvoes. This is the first time in the war that I am flying over the English coastline, confident and ready for the coming action.

The visibility is good, and we can even observe trains moving along the railway lines. Hans gives me a signal and points ahead. In the distance there are black smoke pillars reaching up to our altitude of 5,000m – that must be London.

Very soon we have reached the outer AA gun belt of the capital. The Brits are shooting unpleasantly well, and the whole formation becomes restless. It is now hardly possible to hold my position and I have to devote my whole attention to flying to avoid colliding with other aircraft. All this is completely new to me, and I have no idea how under these circumstances I'm going to follow my own tactics. There is nothing for it but to remain in the middle of the 'big heap'. The AA fire is furious, the shells are continuously exploding all around, above and below us. The surprising thing about it is that all our aircraft are flying on, apparently unscathed. Apart from that the AA fire seems to me an indication that there are no fighters in our vicinity. I am scared of them like the plague . . .

With uncanny inevitability the whole big formation pushes forward over the great city. Ahead I can already see the first bombs falling, and then it is my turn to press the red release button: it is simpler in level formation bombing. The aircraft makes its usual jump of relief and we look down. The Thames bends, the docks and the whole colossal city lie spread out before us like a giant map.

Then come the explosions of our bombs which we observe while banking in a wide turn eastwards, then south. It must be terrible down there. We can see many conflagrations caused by previous bombing raids. The effect of our own attack is an enormous cloud of smoke and dust that shoots up into the sky like a broad moving strip. One cannot imagine that a town or a people could endure this continuous crushing burden for long.

He contrasts this daylight attack with a night mission:

7 October 1940

Night raid on London 0130–1410 hours. The Luftwaffe has changed its tactics. We are no longer flying in large closed formations or even singly in daytime against the British Isles because the losses have become unbearably high. Instead, the aim of wearing down the enemy is now to be achieved by raids of larger formations at night, in exactly the same manner as the British have already tried experimentally over Germany . . .

It is pitch black as we fly into the night. All this is something quite new for us, and that is why we have made especially thorough preparations. For navigational aids we have light and radio beacons. Their positions and identification signals are known to us, and Hans makes a really good job of it all. Already, after flying over the second radio and light beacon . . . we are able to determine the wind direction and speed accurately, and make the necessary course corrections.

We have been instructed to determine our own bearings for further navigation, the procedure being to tune in to known radio beacons with our direction-finder and then measure the direction relative to these transmitters. These values are then transferred on to a map where the points of intersection of any two such base lines would indicate our position at the time. Accurate observation of the elapsed time also makes it possible to calculate our true ground speed and estimate the time to the target.

We arrive over the British coast right on the dot, and are greeted by searchlights which seem to be meandering in a desultory fashion around the sky. Even when they do light up one of our aircraft they do not hold it, but continue playing their searching game. We are flying at 7,000m, and our machine has been sprayed sooty black; it would seem that in this garb we are not visible to the searchlights. That sets our minds at rest, and I continue along the planned route north of the Thames. Ahead the sky is lit up by anti-aircraft fire, and it is soon like a thunderstorm all around us as well. But it is not all one-sided: we can see uninterrupted flashes on the ground, the explosions of bombs dropped by our companions.

One can easily tell the difference between anti-aircraft guns and bomb explosions: while the guns produce only a short flash, a bomb explosion initially gives off a brighter flash, which then slowly burns out. At least that is how it looks to us from our height.

On the way back, after having dropped our bombs in the target area, we are caught by the anti-aircraft guns and this time they seem to be aiming directly at us. In no time at all we are exposed to a furious fire that forces me to fly some violent evasive manoeuvres. However that does not seem to help any, and then I realize that they are not shooting at individual targets but are firing a barrage, covering a predetermined space in the sky in the hope that one shell would hit something. The deadly flashes appear at all heights around us and the minutes seem to be dragging endlessly. We turn south and then east, and manage to get out of the shooting in one piece.

I throttle back our engines and begin slowly to lose height. We are still over the British mainland and have to keep our wits about us. But all goes well and soon we cross the coast, marked by a line of searchlights. It almost looks as if they are waving us goodbye.

Then Hans gives me the correct bearing, and Hein asks if he can play some music. Why not? He switches on Radio Hilversum, and accompanied by cheerful entertaining sounds we cross the North Sea.

Although the 'Battle of Britain' was officially over by 1941, it was business as usual for aircrews on both sides. They continued to fly the same sorties, mount the same raids and mix in the same dogfights as before.

HOWARD SQUIRE, RAF

I was climbing out over Kent towards Boulogne, for a patrol over France. In finger four formation for only the second time, I was the last man in the right flank. Eventually turning down sun for a run towards Calais and Dunkirk, we encountered no flak, but soon an enemy aircraft, which I suspected to be a decoy, rapidly crossed the Squadron's path from left to right. My No 1 immediately peeled off right to intercept and I was forced to follow him down, despite my suspicions, and immediately lost him. In fact, realizing this he had rejoined the Squadron and I found myself alone. Checking for enemy aircraft and unable to locate my colleagues, I turned for home, weaving as I went.

Despite my precautions, a huge bang suddenly shook the airframe, shattering the canopy. Seeing tracer flying past, I realized I had been jumped and immediately rolled the aircraft, pulling the stick hard back, which caused me to black out. When I awoke, the aircraft was in a steep dive, so I started an aileron turn, looking out behind me. Seeing nothing, I began to pull out, but immediately felt more thumping as the unseen German scored more hits. Diving again without being attacked, I was forced to belly-land the aircraft as my engine began to stop.

BOB HAYWARD, RCAF

On February 14 we celebrated our change to Spitfire IXbs by destroying an Me110 at the Hun's advance refuelling base at St Andrew de Leure for the almost nightly bombing of London – no bombing for several nights after; very satisfying.

HEINZ KNOKE, LUFTWAFFE

'Patrol Area Dover-Ashford-Canterbury.' So run our operation orders. 'The milk-run' is what old timers in the Flight call it.

Knoke flew an Me109 on raids across Kent during the summer of 1941.
Here he describes a routine patrol, which was his first mission.

After briefing is over, everyone goes to sleep in armchairs until
breakfast. I go outside, much too excited to sleep, and pace up and
down among the aircraft until I become bored. Back in the crew-
room I try to read. After I have been on ten missions I may be able
to sleep too, like the rest of the boys.

Senior Lieutenant Rech gets into his life jacket at 0750 hours. 'All
right, fellows; let's go! Outside, everyone!' The aircraft are wheeled
out in front of the bays.

0755 hours. I have put on parachute harness. Mechanics give me
a hand adjusting the straps.

0758 hours. I find the excitement terrific. The Chief has raised his
hand. Canopies slam closed. Contact! The engine roars into life. We
taxi across the field. In a few minutes the flight is airborne.

We head west, keeping down low over the water. Radio silence is
maintained; the only sound is the monotonous drone of the engine.

A grey streak looms ahead: the English coast. We cross it north
of Deal.

[The formation] flies inland for several minutes, following the
railway tracks towards Canterbury. There is no traffic. People
glance up at us, no doubt taking us for Spitfires in the haze.

Suddenly we encounter flak, coming up at us from the left. The
tracers come up in orange-coloured chains, and look like pearl
necklaces as they vanish into the clouds beyond us.

The Chief whips his aircraft round and dives after some target:
I cannot make out what it is. My wingman also dives towards the
ground, firing. I see it is a flak emplacement, sandbags round a
20mm pompom gun. Tracers flash right ahead, coming up at me. I
set down the nose and fly low across an open field. I never get to the
point of firing. It is all I can do not to lose sight of Grunert. At any
moment Spitfires may come swooping upon us out of the haze.

The flight resumes formation and heads east. I have not fired a single round. It makes me feel really foolish. True, I was much too excited to have hit anything. I must learn to keep more calm.

There are fighter stations to the north of us, at Ramsgate and Margate. This time no Spitfires or Hurricanes appear. But suppose they were to come? I am at the rear of the flight formation, and it is always the end man who is caught . . .

We spend some time circling over the sea between Folkestone and Dover. The Tommy does not fly in such dirty weather.

His next task was to strafe an RAF station:

Today we were able to carry out a low-level attack on the Tommy airfield near Ramsgate. The weather kept us down to tree-top height.

We took off on the first raid at 0715 hours. Grunert and I chose for our target the fuel dumps on the fighter-station. No aircraft are visible. We strike at the airfield again and again, firing at every moving object. They put up some light flak, but their defences are weak. A number of the fuel drums are on fire by the time we finish.

We return for a second raid at 1000 hours. This time I spot a flak emplacement at the west-end of the runway. I come in to attack it from a height of only ten feet above the ground. But the Tommies stand firm, and open up at me. Their fire passes close to my head; my fire lands in their protecting sandbags. I come in for two more runs at the target. My third attack is successful, and I see my 20mm shells bursting on the gun. The number-one gunner pitches out of the seat.

Suddenly the radio shouts: 'Spitfires!'

Six or eight of them come closing in on us from the north. Not knowing exactly what to do, I keep close behind Grunert. There is a general mix-up that lasts for several minutes. My comrades warn each other by radio when the Tommies are about to attack. Grunert reminds me to stay by him.

We are at an altitude of only a few feet. My left wing-tip almost scrapes the tree tops when I whip my aircraft round after Grunert. A Spitfire just overhead flashes past. There is another one, staying for a few seconds in my sights, and I immediately open fire. It immediately takes cover in the low overcast.

'Got it!' shouts somebody: I think it is Barkhorn. A Spitfire goes down to crash on the other side of the embankment. The bastards can make such infernally tight turns; there seems to be no way of nailing them. Grunert spends several minutes trying to catch two of the Tommies flying close together; but they always break away and vanish into the overcast.

Fuel is running low: it is time to go home. I expect to see the red warning light at any moment. It is the same with the others . . .

It was understandably unpleasant to receive such a visit from the Luftwaffe.

DON KINGABY, RAF

On one occasion, after finishing a patrol, I had just landed at Manston and was walking away from my aircraft when a formation of Messerschmitts made a lightning attack on the airfield. I threw myself to the ground as I saw the flashes and felt the thud of the bullets hammer into the earth around me. I was extremely lucky to get away from this attack with only one smashed finger – it was the only wound I received throughout the whole of the war.

With only the Channel separating the two sides, retaliation was often swift:

HEINZ KNOKE, LUFTWAFFE

Tommy paid us a return visit. Blenheims and Spitfires have been coming over all day long.

It started in the early dawn at 0400 hours, as we were driving out to the airfield. A number of Hurricanes came sweeping over and strafed our maintenance hangar. We climb to 22,000ft. There is not a cloud in sight. We are dazzled by the sun . . . I notice what I think may be enemy aircraft, until I realize that they are only drops of oil on my windshield.

Suddenly Barkhorn whips round, heading back the way we have come. The Hurricanes are on our tails: it is the one place I never thought to look. They try to attack. We pull up in a long, almost vertical climb, then we swing sharply to the left, which brings us back on to their tails. They make off for the open sea, but our speed is greater. Inside of two minutes they are in range.

The dogfight is on. There is wild confusion, in which we all mill around in a mad whirl. I find myself on the tail of the Tommy, and trying to stay there. He has me spotted, and pulls round to the left into the sun. I climb after him with every gun blazing, but I am dazzled by the sun. Blast! I try using my hand to shield my eyes, but it is no good. He has got away. I am so angry I could kick myself. I have to give it up. And to think that this might have been my first kill!

In future I must take care to wear sunglasses.

Both air forces pursued the conflict with unrelenting vigour:

JOHNNIE JOHNSON, RAF

We flew and fought hard during that epic summer [1941]. Douglas [Bader] was a great and inspiring leader whose fruity language in the air was a joy to hear. He took time to teach us the intricate art of air fighting. His idea of an afternoon off was to take one or two of us over the Channel hoping to come across Adolf Galland and some of his chaps, then based at Abbeville in the Pas de Calais.

ALAN SMITH, RAF

2 July 1941: We were doing an offensive patrol over France

combined with bomber escort to Lille. There was a great deal of opposition and a considerable amount of dog-fighting during which the Squadron destroyed three and damaged two. My first confirmed enemy aircraft destroyed – an Me109, which shed various bits and pieces of metal after two long bursts from astern. It was pouring heavy smoke and proceeded almost vertically downwards. A further Me109, which came in to attack me, overshot and I got in a quick burst that did a certain amount of damage. As always in these dogfights, the sky was full of aircraft one moment and practically devoid of them the next.

DON KINGABY, RAF

On 2 July 1941, early in the afternoon, my Squadron was returning from a sweep over Lille, when two aircraft which I thought were Hurricanes dived down in front of my section. I realized, too late, they were Messerschmitt 109s. The next moment two more Me109s came diving down and obviously the first two had been bait for us, while the second pair were supposed to shoot us up. However I whipped in behind this pair and fired a long burst into each of them, scoring direct hits. I broke off immediately, suspecting more Me109s were on their way down. As I climbed away I saw two more Me109s diving, confirming my suspicions, and far below just had time to see my two Me109s splash into the sea. Satisfyingly I saw at least one parachute open.

LARRY ROBILLARD, RCAF

On 2 July 1941, [Adolf] Galland and I (we subsequently learned) met in the air with pretty dire results for both of us. I saw his Me109F attacking some Blenheim bombers and got on to his tail. After a steep dive and some steep turns I got in close, fired and saw strikes on the right hand side of his cockpit. I was about to finish him off when I saw a flash of other fighters in the sun and I had to break hard into four Me109s coming at me head on.

They approached very fast. Their leader was firing at me, and I fired at him and hit him. Somehow we missed colliding and I turned and dived for the ground and safety. Suddenly I felt a great wallop in my back and part of my wing fell off. My Spitfire went into a vicious spin, completely out of control, and I blacked out. When I came to, the ground was coming up at a great rate of knots. I pulled the ripcord, the parachute opened, but somehow my legs were caught in the lines and I was going down head-first! After much struggling I got in the correct position and landed by a railway embankment with 109s circling overhead.

OMER LEVESQUE, RCAF

On the afternoon of 23 November 1941, we had just crossed the coast at Boulogne when one of the boys warned of an impending attack from six o'clock. Our section turned to port, pulling a high G-force when, to my surprise, I saw an aircraft above at ten o'clock and a parachute floating under my left wing. This aircraft did not in any way resemble a Me109. Then I saw more with radial engines and enemy markings. I fired a short burst at one of these strange fighters and white smoke poured from under his fuselage and I followed him down in a left-hand dive and stayed with him through some wild manoeuvring. I fired several times and last saw him going steeply down, pouring smoke and on fire. Then I fired at another, but broke off when I was attacked. Fortunately our Wing Leader and his section came to my rescue . . .

This was my first encounter with the redoubtable FW-190.

HUGH GODEFROY, RCAF

One day when the controller reported a lot of enemy activity over Pas de Calais I thought I saw sparks coming out of my engine. On closer inspection I realized they were going the other way. Tracer! I broke violently and saw my number two, Brian Hodgkinson, going down in flames. I was in the midst of a swarm of Me109s.

Turning and twisting, I fired at every 109 that came in front of me until I ran out of ammunition. For what seemed an eternity I held my Spitfire in tight, shuddering turns to avoid being shot down. Eventually, I pulled the stick back into my guts and kicked the Spitfire into a spin. At 15,000ft I recovered from the spin and continued down in a spiral dive. At 10,000ft I started a pull-out and headed for the white cliffs of Dover – when I saw them they looked like the pearly gates. On landing at Biggin I found that of the twelve pilots who had taken off, eight were missing.

Being posted as missing did not necessarily mean a pilot was dead. If he could survive the ordeal of baling out, he might manage to make it home, with or without assistance:

HUGH DUNDAS, RAF

A fighter pilot's most significant, and most important combat experience is when, for the first time, he is comprehensively shot down and manages to survive. He learns from that, as from nothing else.

ALAN DEERE, RAF

It has always been said by my contemporaries that I bore a charmed life, but if I had not had a Spitfire strapped to my bottom for the whole of my operational career, I doubt that I would have survived. Tough as it was, the Spitfire could not be expected to survive the treatment to which I regularly subjected it. It causes me some embarrassment therefore to record that we parted company on no less than nine occasions. The fact that I survived was thanks to a great deal of luck and the reliability of the Irvine parachute. Nevertheless, I can say, I think with justification and not a little pride, that as a partnership, we accounted for 22 enemy aircraft destroyed, with numerous other either 'probably destroyed' or 'damaged'.

FRANK CAREY, RAF

On 10 May 1940, after an intense period of fighting with plenty of
good fortune, I was shot down, slightly wounded in the leg, near
Wavre, to be snatched from under the nose of the Germans by an
enterprising Belgian Army patrol. About a month later in company
with three other slightly shop-soiled RAF pilots near St Nazaire
we came across a forlorn Bristol Bombay absolutely asking to be
brought back to the UK . . .

HUGH GODEFROY, RCAF

My Merlin 61 engine finally let me down. It caught fire returning
from Normandy to England and without time to give a mayday I
baled out in mid-Channel. Fortunately, a ship was passing, a man
saw me and gave the alarm, and soon I was safe on board.

DENIS CROWLEY-MILLING, RAF

Flying on sweeps and escort operations over northern France, I was
shot down in August 1941.

I managed to evade capture by the Germans, made contact
with the underground and came down the escape route via Paris,
Marseilles and the Pyrenees. Unfortunately I was captured in
Spain and spent three months in [prison], where I became ill with
paratyphoid. On being released, and on recovering, I returned
to the UK to rejoin 610 Squadron, taking command, once again,
of my old flight.

DENYS GILLAM, RAF

We were based at Valley in Wales. Some bored pilot wrote to our
Honorary Air Commodore, Winston Churchill, complaining that the
Squadron had been out of the front line for too long. As a result,
in September 1941, we were sent to Manston in Kent where, in our
cannon-firing Hurricanes, we undertook low-level attacks against
enemy shipping in the Channel. We had to contend with a lot of flak,

both from the German merchant vessels and their E-boats, and we lost a lot of casualties. The length of the Squadron tour as Channel Stop was supposed to be three weeks, but we were at Manston from 12 September 1941 to 23 November 1941. I myself was hit by flak, baled out and was rescued from the sea just off Dunkirk.

ADOLF GALLAND, LUFTWAFFE

Early in the afternoon (of 21 June 1941) I foolishly took off alone to intercept an incursion north of Boulogne. A single Spitfire appeared in front of me which, shooting at very close range, promptly exploded. My Me109 then received hits from a second Spitfire; I got splinters in my head and arm. With burning fuel in my cockpit, I had to bail out, but could not jettison the canopy and, trying to climb out with it hanging open, my parachute became caught in the rear section, flames now blowing over me. Just as I was about to take off my chute, the radio mast saved me and I was out. After expert treatment over a glass of brandy and a cigar, I received the award of the Swords to the Knight's Cross and was forbidden by Hitler to fly any more combat missions for the time being.

If they were captured, they were often received with courtesy and hospitality by fellow professionals. One pilot was both victor and vanquished within a short space of time:

PADDY BARTHROPP, RAF

After the fight we drove to the crash site and afterwards I met the pilot at the local police station. He was wearing a smart pair of flying boots, which I persuaded him to change for my shoes, and I still have them to this day.

Later I was posted as a flight commander to 122 Squadron and on 17 May 1942, I was shot down by Karl Willius, who later told me he was extremely angry because I had just killed his best friend, one Rolf Ermichen. I baled out and was picked up by German soldiers who relieved me of my gold half-hunter watch and my silver cigarette-case. That night Willius visited me in the jail at St Omer and before he left asked me if I had any complaints or requests. I told him about the watch and cigarette case and he muttered something about army bastards. A few hours later the watch, cigarette case, some black sausages and half a dozen pints of lager beer were delivered to my cell with a card that said 'With the compliments of the Luftwaffe'.

The comradeship of flying was a tremendous bond between the opposing sides. The Luftwaffe was a superb fighting force whose pilots showed enormous skill, courage and chivalry, and they were greatly respected by their enemy. As well as sharing professional ability, however, these men had something else in common – they were reduced to mutual exhaustion by the constant pressure of risking their lives. As Hitler's priorities shifted, Luftwaffe operations in the West became steadily less intensive, and the fighting – successful for the British, inconclusive for the Germans – entered a quieter phase.

HEINZ LANGE, LUFTWAFFE

On the whole, the battle was conducted fairly, neither side shooting aircrew hanging from parachutes, but the strain on our nerves was immense. After the first few weeks, the wings had rest days and could be sent home until being returned to standby. Then we would meet at the Rio Bar in Lille, a well-known bar which the English had used before us. As the weather worsened, the crews were near the end of their strength and the battle drew to a close, but we had lost a lot of friends, many of whom had been [sent] to captivity in Canada. In a way we felt sorry for them, but later on there were times when we envied them.

3

BOMBER OFFENSIVE

Bomber crews had an entirely different war to that of their counterparts in fighters. At the start of the conflict neither side had a truly modern or efficient aircraft, equivalent to the Hurricane, Spitfire or Me109. Neither was capable of delivering a large-bomb load to a distant enemy city – but neither sought to do so.

Despite the destruction of civilian targets in Spain during the 'dress rehearsal' for World War II, the protagonists initially avoided such casualties, and this attitude changed only after the first 12 months. Bombers entered the war by attacking enemy shipping, widened their scope to include ports and factories, and finally – deliberately, for the former stricture was stood on its head – set out to obliterate large centres of population. Originally it was feared that this practice would stiffen morale and fuel the enemy's will to fight. Ironically, it was later pursued in order to undermine that same morale. It was, in any case, difficult to target military facilities without causing civilian deaths, and after the tit-for-tat raids on London and Berlin in autumn 1940, Hitler ordered his flyers to abandon any remaining scruples. His enemy was quick to follow suit.

The bomber war began during 1940 and was of great importance to the British, and Allied, war effort. At a time when German armies were triumphant on all fronts, it gave Britain a unique opportunity to hit back at the enemy's heartland. As the tide turned against Hitler it was believed that bombing would hasten Germany's collapse. In fact the Allied offensive, like the Blitz, failed significantly in its objectives: it did not destroy the enemy's industry, which actually increased production, and it did not cow the population, whose will to resist was enhanced. Only when it targeted, and decimated, Germany's fuel supplies did it achieve a major effect.

Bombing was highly expensive in lives and machines. The heavier a bomb-load and the more well-armed a plane, the slower it would travel. Finding a balance between speed, range, armour and payload was the crucial challenge facing designers, but, with the development of the Lancaster in 1941 and the arrival of the American B-17 the following year, the Allies obtained two aircraft excellently adapted for the task in hand. The greatest problem for bomber fleets was their vulnerability – by day or night – to highly efficient German fighter defences. Their own fighters lacked sufficient fuel to escort them farther than western Europe and as a result their losses were immense, at one time requiring the suspension of operations by the USAAF. In 1944 the situation improved with the introduction of the long-range P-47 and P-51 Mustangs, which could fly all the way to a target. Nevertheless the risks – and the losses – remained very high to the end. RAF Bomber Command, which formed less than 10 per cent of Britain's armed forces, suffered 25 per cent of the casualties.

Early and bitter experience had driven the RAF to bomb largely at night, though this had frequently meant missing the right targets or hitting the wrong ones. Important radar developments, including GEE and 'Oboe', enabled instruments to locate an objective and saved the crew from lengthy, fuel-guzzling passes over the target, while clouds of 'chaff' were dropped to disorient the enemy's own radar. The USAAF, whose bomber fleets were bigger and more well-armed, flew by day, seeking to force its way by weight of numbers and dint of firepower. This pattern of Anglo-American operations remained unchanged throughout the war.

The tonnage of bombs dropped on Germany and her occupied territories by Allied planes was colossal (in 1944, the last full year of war, it came to 914,637). Whatever the moral arguments regarding this level of destruction, there can be no doubting the enormous, deeply moving courage of those who flew the missions.

By the summer of 1940 the bomber war, with its characteristic aspects – formation-flying, flak and searchlights, and the sight of other aircraft crashing in flames – was already well-established:

ROD LEAROYD, RAF

On the night of 12 August 1940 we took off with four other aircraft and headed for the Dortmund-Ems Canal. To achieve success we needed to approach from a direction which took us through the most concentrated lane of anti-aircraft defences.

We stooged around the target area until the precise time for our attack arrived. The precise timing was important, especially for us as No 5 in the line up; apart from not interfering with the other aircraft we would, if late, risk being blown up by the leader's ten-minute delayed-action missile.

As I dived our Hampden down to 150ft in a wide curve to line up with the canal, I realized that the searchlights were going to present almost as much menace as the flak. The reception for all of the aircraft ahead of me was severe, two being brought down. I ducked my head below the panel and flew on instruments, taking quick looks outside to check that I was on the right line.

I was dazzled by the searchlights and we were repeatedly hit by gunfire, but aided by calls from the bomb aimer managed to reach the target and soon I was very happy to hear yells on the intercom of 'Bomb Away!' from the bomb aimer Flight Officer Lewis and, from the upper and lower gunners Sergeant Ellis and Aircraftsman Rich that it was on target. As we jinked away from the area we found that the hydraulic system was out of action and that we had lost a few large pieces from the main plane. Fortunately no one was injured.

I managed to get the aircraft back to Scampton, but as both landing flaps and undercarriage indicators were out of action, I toured the area to use up fuel and waited for daylight before a comparatively uneventful landing.

Young aircrew were able to build up valuable experience on short-distance, comparatively easy objectives.

JACK V WATTS, RCAF

We had Whitley bombers, with Rolls-Royce Merlin engines, and on
2 September 1940 I flew my first operation when we bombed Ostend
– considered a 'nursery' target for new crews.

Some inexperienced crew members were able to suppress natural fears
by concentrating on the task in hand. One, whose cool bravery later
earned him the VC, remembered:

BILL REID, RAF

I was flying the usual operational sorties over Germany and reacted
like most raw recruits in being rather tense until we had our target
instructions. Beyond this point one had so much to do that there was
no time to think of the dangers ahead.

On the night of 12–13 November 1940, Leonard Cheshire piloted a Whitley
bomber in a raid on Cologne. Having crossed half of Europe, they found
their objective obscured by cloud. As was common in these circumstances,
they had a secondary target – in this case the marshalling-yards of the
city's important railway station. Severely damaged while on its approach
to this, the plane completed its mission and was brought home by the skill
of its crew.

LEONARD CHESHIRE, RAF

I learned that night yet another lesson: I was as dependent upon
my crew's skill, courage and dedication, as they were on mine.
Flight Sergeant Henry Davidson, the wireless operator, had taken
the full force of the blast and his face was charred black, leaving
him totally blind. His ordeal was made all the worse when another
shell came through the cockpit, adding a roaring wind to his already
considerable problems. It also temporarily stunned me and made
me think we were going vertically down out of control. Despite the
unspeakable agony Davidson suffered he insisted on returning to

his wireless set in order to try to maintain contact with base for the five-hour struggle home.

Flak was not, of course, the only peril for the bomber crews. Enemy fighters were even more dangerous.

DIGGER KYLE, RAF

On 7 March 1941 I led a daylight low-level attack at Squadron strength, on a steel works in Holland. We attacked in two waves at very short intervals. There was some flak but we were almost on the deck and it was fairly ineffective. We split up on withdrawal and I was picked up by two 109s. They tried for about 15 minutes to shoot us down but failed because we flew only a few feet above the sea and my rear gunner judged his order to turn exactly. We watched tracer going above us and wide but didn't get one hit. I have never flown so accurately and it seemed a long time.

All aircraft got back to base but we had three crash landings due to hydraulic damage.

While the RAF pursued the war over Germany and the Continent, their opponents continued to attack British targets:

JOHN CUNNINGHAM, RAF

On the night of 3–4 April 1941, south-west of the Needles, flying a Beaufighter with my operator Jimmy Rawnsley, we got a radar contact at 7,000ft range. The target was jinking, and seemed to be following no set pattern, flying in a generally haphazard way southwards. We closed in, slowing to a point directly beneath the target so that I could identify it clearly. At 2,000ft range I identified the aircraft as a Heinkel 111 and slowly climbed up to close beneath the enemy aircraft, then slid back so that I could bring my guns to bear on the target.

All around us were huge piles of moonlit cumulo-nimbus cloud.

A violent thunderstorm was raging in the clouds beneath us and with every flash of lightning we could see the clear outline of the Heinkel. Surely their gunners must see us at any second.

Slowly the He111 sank into my sights as I eased the Beaufighter into position to get an accurate shot. I could see his pale blue exhaust flames sprouting from the engine cowlings.

Immediately I opened fire there was an enormous flash and the Heinkel exploded in a ball of fire. We ploughed through the flying debris collecting a number of unpleasant hits, but a quick check of my instruments showed all systems functioning normally.

The spinning, burning He111 had shed a wing and spun vertically into the moonlit thunderclouds below leaving a trail of flame behind it. Its instant destruction in the midst of the violent storm was awe-inspiring.

Although the bomber offensive had not yet hit its stride, raids were frequent. Berlin, the most important political target of the war, required a gruelling journey of eight to ten hours, and its defences were formidable.

KEN BATCHELOR, RAF

In a Wellington Ic of 9 Squadron we set course for Berlin on the moonlit night of the 9 April 1941. Over Holland the solid searchlight 'barrier' running down from Emden was busily coning other aircraft. The apex of the cones were filled with flak or the tracer of night fighters. Avoiding a weaving master we escaped but saw five aircraft go down in flames and burning on the ground. Berlin, as clear as day, had searchlight cones holding some aircraft. Suddenly, a master caught us, immediately joined by about 30 others and then flak was bursting loudly all around us. For an interminable time we were pasted right across that huge city, the smoke puffs of the yellow bursts lit by the searchlights and the near concussions bumping us continuously. A night to remember but not the only one by any means.

DEREK TULLOCH, RAF

During the course of my 76 operations we experienced many frightening events and on many occasions were lucky to survive. As rear gunner I was usually first to get sight of attacking enemy aircraft and my job was to co-ordinate defence of our aircraft by returning the attack with my guns, and at the same time to give discretional instructions to the pilot, who often had to rely on me for information in the case of attacks from astern. The standard evasive action in the case of fighter attack was for the pilot to 'corkscrew' the aircraft – make a violent turn to left or right – and this added considerably to the gunners' difficult job of hitting fast-moving attacking fighters. Most of these combats were at night, and thus the task of actually hitting or bringing down an enemy fighter was a difficult one to say the least.

Flak was a constant danger to all bomber aircraft, as was collision at night, and even the danger of bombs falling from higher aircraft above. On the night of 23 March whilst over Berlin we had already collected some flak damage when we were hit by an incendiary bomb, which fell from another aircraft above us. It came right through the roof and started a fire in the fuselage. If it had not been for some quick thinking by our wireless operator, who put the fire out, the aircraft would have broken in half and we would have become a victim of our own bombing!

A vital member of any bomber crew was the navigator. One of them remembered his outlook when flying on raids:

JOHN BENISON, RAF

Losses on Halifaxes were heavy at that time, sometimes 10 per cent or more on a single night raid; mostly caused by night fighters for which a bomber on the edge, or outside, the main stream was the easiest target to track and shoot down. It soon struck me that crews which regularly arrived back shot up by fighters, or survived few operations, seemed to be those with below average navigators. Thereafter I aimed to navigate over enemy territory towards where the densest mass of bombers would be. We completed a tour of 24 operations in good order and were never shot at by a night fighter. I like to think that my navigation may have played some part in this!

Not all targets were cities. A major objective in the naval war was the sinking of the battleship *Tirpitz* which, after a lengthy search, was discovered hidden in a Norwegian fjord. The RAF took on the task, as some of the participants recall:

REG LANE, RCAF

On 23 April 1942, 35 Squadron (RAF) moved to Kinloss, Scotland. Not until we arrived were we told that we were to carry out the second of three attacks against the German battleship *Tirpitz*. The attack was to be at masthead height, dropping special mines between the ship and the wall of the fjord, near Trondjheim, Norway, to which the ship was moored. I flew to Norway in formation with another Canadian in the Squadron, Flying Officer DP MacIntyre. We were flying Halifax Mk IIs.

I followed MacIntyre into the target after letting down to approximately 200ft near Trondjheim. We were heavily engaged by the light anti-aircraft defences, and I watched in horror as MacIntyre was hit and burst into flames. We also were under severe attack with shells hitting the aircraft. The Germans were aware that we were coming and had set off smoke generators to hide the ship. Notwithstanding the defences, we did a timed run from a small island at the entrance to the fjord, dropped the mines and then pulled up immediately to slide over the top of the hill to the left in the hope of escaping the guns. This worked. The aircraft had been severely damaged, but fortunately none of the crew were injured. Sadly we lost several aircraft that night.

DON BENNETT, RAF

While with No 10 Squadron, based at Leeming, on the 27 April 1942,
I was piloting Halifax 1041 'B-Baker', one of 32 Halifaxes from Nos
10, 35 and 76 Squadrons who set out from Lossiemouth, detailed
to destroy the German battleship, *Tirpitz*, in Aasfjord, Norway. I
reached the target area carrying five 1,000lb special mines, having
earlier been hit by heavy flak in which my tail gunner was severely
wounded and our starboard wing set on fire.

We were determined to make our drop, and I pulled the Halifax
round and, passing over the *Tirpitz* again, let them go. I swung
round with the idea of heading east towards Sweden. As I told the
crew to get their parachutes on I realized we were approaching a
mountain range far too high for the crippled plane. I held her while
the crew jumped and then jumped myself, just as the burning wing
finally came away. I landed very quickly in deep snow, and found my
wireless operator. With the help of Norwegian Patriots we made it to
Sweden and were back at base inside one month.

It was to be more than two years before the great ship was finally sent to
the bottom, but it would be Bomber Command that finished the job.

* * *

By this stage in the war one of Britain's most effective weapons – the
Mosquito fighter-bomber – was in action:

ROY RALSTON, RAF

At the request of the navy, we were briefed to bomb two 10,000 ton
blockade runners making for Bordeaux. Our routing was Marham
in Norfolk to Cornwall, then down to sea level, leading six Mosquitos
in formation round Brittany to the Bay of Biscay where we found
the ships in the mouth of the River Gironde. We carried out, and
photographed, an excellent bombing attack, but Flight Lieutenant

Bristow was shot down. Due to the length of the trip we could just make England with little to spare and by this time it would be dark.

Base were to make arrangements with RAF Predannock in Cornwall to be ready to bring us in as quickly as possible. In the event we could make no contact with the Station, went into distress signals 'mayday' and flashing our navigation lights, when the flarepath was put on, and we landed safely only to receive a rocket from the Station Commander. Whilst we had been away on the trip all communications with the West Country had been suspended as Operation Torch, the invasion of Africa, was being launched that night.

For aircrews, this operation meant facing the same old dangers in a comparatively exotic setting, though this could have advantages – one Canadian flyer baled out into the Mediterranean; he could not possibly have survived a similar immersion in the North Sea.

JACK V WATTS, RCAF

10 November 1942, was my 22nd birthday and my last operation with 100 Squadron. I was navigator of a Halifax on a night mission and we had just released our big bombs over Tobruk when we received a direct hit from an anti-aircraft shell. It got us under the bomb bay and caused quite an explosion as some of our smaller bombs burst. Our two port engines caught fire and the stricken Halifax headed out to sea and couldn't be turned back. The Captain ordered his crew to bail-out. I opened the escape hatch and out we went. After my parachute opened I saw our bomber crash into the sea.

I had no Mae West, and as soon as I hit the water I took off all my clothes and started to swim towards Tobruk guided by a huge fire. I figured that I had about a five-mile swim, but after an hour or so the fire was put out and I navigated by the stars. After swimming for about four more hours I reached the shore.

It was still dark and the beach was very rocky. I crawled up among the rocks and found a sort of cave. It was really only a big crevice but since I was in enemy occupied territory, it was my home for three days and nights – without clothes – until I had to move to get water and food, otherwise I would have been too weak to save myself.

After about half a mile I found a deserted building and, inside, a German uniform, some water and a can of tomato juice. Eventually I went to sleep and the next morning I was awakened by the sound of a truck and English voices from three military policemen who made me a fine big breakfast.

However, most of Bomber Command's efforts continued to be devoted to Europe.

ROLAND HAMMERSLEY, RAF

Every operation was eventful, some much worse than others. If it wasn't the enemy it could be something potentially as disastrous, like a hydraulic failure or a hung-up bomb (we had both on Juvisy marshalling yards, 18 April 1944), or loss of an engine (Schweinfurt, 26 April 1944).

The elite of Bomber Command were the Pathfinders – the crews that flew ahead of the main force and circled the target, dropping flares to guide the planes that followed. They remained over the target longer than anyone else and the defenders made particular efforts to destroy them. They had a dedication and an *esprit de corps* that marked them out as the bravest of the brave, as acknowledged in this account by one of them.

JOHN SEARBY, RAF

I had finished my tour of duty in March 1943, but, on one of his rare visits to a frontline squadron, Air Marshal Harris sent for me. He was in the course of inspecting the airmen's dining hall, in company with Air Vice Marshal Cochrane, and the encounter was brief. He informed me I was to take command of No 83 Pathfinder Squadron immediately – to leave Syerston, where I had been very happy, for Wyton, as soon as I could hand over. There was no discussion – no question of my taking the usual end-of-tour leave – and within 48 hours I took command of 83 Squadron with Air Vice Marshal Bennett as my new boss. The previous Commanding Officer had been killed over Dortmund a few days earlier; we must have passed each other because I attacked that target the same night but he, alas, didn't make it back to base. It was a rough night, with intense heavy flak and plenty of 'freelance' fighters operating in the target area: we were within an ace of colliding with a Focke-Wulf 190 who passed across the nose of the Lancaster – possibly more frightened than we were!

The Pathfinders were a dedicated lot – first in at all the performances – braving the flak, searchlights and other novelties in their effort to mark the aiming points for the hundreds of heavy bombers following on behind. All were volunteers and I was fortunate to join a band of stalwarts whose enthusiasm and devotion to duty led the way. The Bomber Offensive was gathering momentum and the enemy, in turn, was increasing the strength of his twin and single-engined squadrons to oppose us. Krupps Works at Essen was flattened and much more of the Ruhr; all the great cities of the German Reich came under the hammer blows of Bomber Command: Hamburg was taken out in three swift attacks and in the autumn the preliminary attacks began on the enemy's capital city . . . a battle which was to prove the fiercest of all! At Peenemunde we destroyed the greater part of the V Weapons Establishment – thus making possible the assault which opened with D-Day the following June. This was a memorable attack in which I acted the part of Master Bomber, remaining over the target for 45 minutes during which forty of our heavy bombers were destroyed.

As Master Bomber on the Peenemunde attack I remained over

the area for the full duration. Six-hundred heavy bombers
flying in waves attacked the three separate targets at 15 minute
intervals. I arrived five minutes early with my crew and made
a quick reconnaissance, then drew off to await the onslaught.
Subsequently we flew over the aiming points, endeavouring to
correct the marking where necessary and encouraging the main
force to bomb with the greatest possible accuracy. Bombs falling
from above presented a real hazard. In the last half of the attack
the German night fighters arrived in great numbers and the scene
was fantastic with bombers exploding over the target. We were
the last to leave Peenemunde and suffered attack from an Me110
– driven off by my gunners who claimed him as 'damaged' since we
did not see him crash.

Though the Pathfinders were a considerable asset, they could do nothing
to lessen the danger over the target:

ROBERT E MACKETT, RCAF

On the night of 27 September during a raid on Hanover, we
encountered very strong searchlight activity at 18,000ft coupled with
heavy and accurate flak.

With outstanding navigation we were able to drop a load of
incendiaries over the target within seconds of the 'drop time', and
still faced such a strength of enemy searchlights that it took violent
evasive action to avoid. Gunners and engineers kept a running
patter of groping searchlights but we were caught with the odd
'Blue Master Beam' that would immediately snap on to us.

We dropped down to 8,000ft before outrunning the searchlight
belt. During these manoeuvres flak tore a hole through the
windscreen, and glass and wind temporarily blinded me. Returning
over the Zuider Zee the rear gunner reported seeing the glow
of Hanover fires, 90 miles to the rear. This was outstanding
crew co-operation.

Night fighters continued to pose the most serious danger – even if they were lacking in experience.

PAUL ZORNER, LUFTWAFFE

My first enemy contact came on 28 July 1942 – a Wellington bomber returning from a raid on Berlin. As I closed in to about 200m he suddenly began to turn and, losing my nerve, I started shooting – much too early! With the bomber crew alerted, the aircraft then made a split S manoeuvre and disappeared into the haze . . .

More accurate shooting could cause very serious difficulties for a plane attempting to get home. This crew was extremely lucky:

MICHAEL BEETHAM, RAF

[On 3 December 1943] Leipzig was the target for our 50 Squadron Lancaster. It was a bitterly cold night at 20,000ft and we were having trouble with our intercom to the two gunners. We had just bombed the target and had turned for home when the rear gunner saw a Ju88 closing rapidly. He tried to warn me but his intercom was frozen; so too, maddeningly, were his four guns.

The mid-upper gunner spotted the Ju88 at about 200 yards and shouted 'Corkscrew port!' as he opened fire. As I pulled the Lancaster round in a violent corkscrew I felt the cannon shells thudding into the port wing. The mid-upper gunner then said he had hit the Ju88 and that it had veered away. When calm returned, an assessment of the damage showed that we were losing fuel from our port wing tank, otherwise we seemed to be flying all right. Fortunately we were able to husband our fuel, and made it back to another airfield.

MURRAY PEDEN, RCAF

Near Gelsenkirchen we were attacked near the target by two German fighters in succession and badly shot up. After the second combat, we struggled home to an emergency aerodrome with two of the crew wounded, and crash-landed, cutting a fully-loaded Lancaster in half in the process. Its crew had been unable to drop their bomb-load after a night fighter shot up the hydraulics. As they saw our Fortress swerving toward their Lanc at high speed, they scattered, and neither their wounded rear gunner nor our wounded crewmen were further injured in the spectacular demolition-derby that resulted – in fact I and my engineer, last to get out and acutely mindful of a still-smoking engine sitting atop 2,000 gallons of 100 octane fuel, left the smouldering wreckage on foot, moving our flying boots at speeds which might still qualify us for Olympics competition could we do a repeat. Three of us received official commendations, but my crew, on the other hand, maintained with some vehemence that I should simply have received the Iron Cross from the Germans for destroying two British bombers in as many seconds!

ROLAND HAMMERSLEY, RAF

About 50 miles short of our target there was an almighty bang right underneath the navigator and I, followed by a cloud of smoke. The pilot commenced to corkscrew, whilst both gunners were firing at the attacking Ju88.

All internal and external lights came on. The rear gunner had been hit and his turret was on fire.

The navigator went back with a fire extinguisher and managed to put out the fire. I followed him down the fuselage and managed to drag the rear gunner out of the damaged turret to dress his wounds. Apart from bullet wounds, he had quite serious burns. The turret was unusable, as was the GEE and H2S. Fortunately my wireless equipment still functioned so I advised base of our predicament and that a doctor and ambulance would be required.

To add to our problems we burst a tyre on landing and the Lancaster slewed off the runway. We ended up facing the control tower with the ambulance in pursuit.

The Ju88 that caused so many problems went down in flames from our gunners' accurate fire. The rear gunner received an immediate DFC.

Even a mission from which an aircraft returned undamaged and with a complete crew could be an extremely stressful experience.

DAVE SHANNON, RAAF

Some 260 aircraft were to attack Munich using 617 Squadron's low-level visual marking technique on a major target deep in the heart of Germany. I was deputy to Leonard Cheshire.

Over the target we met intense flak and searchlight defences, however. Aided by flares dropped by some of the Lancasters, Cheshire's markers were accurately placed and my markers fell on top of those already blazing, intensifying the target for the main force. Climbing away, we were coned in searchlights, with flak exploding all around. It was an exciting ten minutes before I managed to shake them off and ask my navigator, Len Sumpton, for a course to base. Len's laconic reply: 'When I get my night vision back perhaps I'll find my maps, meantime for God's sake fly west!' We arrived back at Manston at dawn with about five minutes' fuel to spare.

To limp home with a damaged plane and an injured crew was a depressingly frequent occurrence.

BILL REID, RAF

Inevitably, my most memorable operational sortie was the one that led to my being awarded the Victoria Cross.

It was 3 November 1943, and we were detailed to attack Dusseldorf. My windscreen was shattered by an Me100 just after crossing the Dutch coast, and I was hit in the head, shoulders and hands. As soon as the Me100 had been driven off, an FW-190 attacked. This time we were strafed from stem to stern.

My navigator was killed, my wireless operator fatally injured, the flight engineer and I were both also hit. With most systems out of commission I had to use memory to fly on to the target and the moon and the pole star to return to England.

Damage to one's own aircraft, the planes of others or even to nearby buildings was commonplace and almost inevitable. Where tons of fuel-filled metal had to be handled skillfully in a crowded environment, mishaps were bound to occur, whether in taking off . . .

VIC AZZARO, RAF

On our second trip our over-enthusiastic flight engineer whipped up the undercarriage before we had got airborne, bringing us back smartly on to the ground on our belly. We went hurtling up the runway at flying speed, in a shower of sparks, shedding bits and pieces in all directions. I turned my turret to the rear and jumped out! The aircraft finished up at the end of the runway in bits.

. . . or, according to the same narrator, while in the air:

It was always very crowded over any target area, particularly on the large raids. On one occasion we collided with a Halifax right over the target. I am not sure if he climbed up to us or whether we landed on him, but his mid-turret scraped all along the length of our bomb door and took the H2S scanner away. I remember thinking that we had enough to contend with over the target without having to try and survive mid-air collisions! Thankfully we got home safely.

. . . or when landing:

DOUGLAS CAMERON, RAF

We ran ourselves very low on fuel and only just managed to make it to Manston, only to find the airfield swarming with Spitfires returning from a sweep over France. Manston being a Fighter Command station, they were somewhat surprised to see the huge form of a Stirling lumbering in, and the fighters scattered out of our way. The moment we touched down both port engines cut out and the starboard engines propelled us off in the direction of parked aircraft. There was nothing we could do. We ploughed straight though a bunch of Spitfires and Beaufighters, writing them off as we went, demolished an armoury, left our undercarriage in the airmens' huts and came to rest with the fuselage resting up against one of the hangers. We were not Manston's most popular visitors that day!

Aircraft were vulnerable, and when over enemy territory a relatively secure and intact plane could turn within seconds into an inferno, or become so damaged that it must be abandoned at once. Despite the horror of these situations, some flyers were later able to recall them with grim humour.

HAMISH MAHADDIE, RAF

Certainly the most memorable sortie in which I was involved was on the night of 1–2 February 1943. Detailed as the 'Y' target – marker for a raid on Cologne, I was piloting Stirling R9273, MG-C. We made it to the target markers, the cloud cover seemed to (indeed did literally) dissolve into thin air. We were suddenly beset by ferocious flak and our intercom system and rear turret were quickly knocked out. To rub salt into the wound, a not-very friendly Junkers 88 promptly turned up and blasted the entire length of our fuselage. My mid-upper air gunner, wireless operator and bomb aimer were all wounded, the 'G' and 'Y' wrecked, aileron controls severed and all navigation aids having been rendered useless, I found myself flying something whose airworthiness rather resembled that of a housebrick!

Thompson, my navigator, performed near-miracles, initially
in first aid. Our flight engineer found and repaired the severed
controls and we were able to limp home, where we counted no less
than 174 cannon shell-holes in the Stirling which was, of course,
promptly re-christened 'C-for-Colander'.

The pressure on pilots during a mission was immense. The man flying the
aircraft might have to decide whether to abort and turn for home, whether
to jettison the bomb-load, or whether damage was serious enough to
warrant abandoning the plane. The courage shown by some pilots in this
situation was magnificent:

SA BOOKER, RAF

The operation to attack the railway marshalling yards at Trappes
should have been just another of the relatively uncomplicated
French and Belgian railway targets that No 4 Group had been
bombing consistently since Easter 1944.

Halifax 'S' for Sugar had spiralled up to join the main stream of
105 four-engine Halifax bombers taking off from numerous airfields
in the Vale of York. After converging to overfly the mandatory
turning points at Basingstoke and Pevensey Bay, [we] crossed the
Channel, flying into France exactly on time, experiencing very little
flak or other opposition throughout the remainder of the route, up
to the outskirts of Paris.

The bombing run into the target area had been quite uneventful
– the weather was almost perfect. No cloud, good visibility and a
brilliant three-quarter moon enabling the air gunners to maintain
a good look-out and immediately report on any unwelcome bombers
converging too dangerously, or even worse, flying with the bomb
doors open.

The target had been clearly marked and the stick of 18,500lb,
delayed action, high explosive bombs were dropped on the cluster
of yellow and white ground markers as instructed by the Master

Bomber circling many thousands of feet below in his twin-engined Mosquito aircraft.

A violent explosion near the aiming point was experienced as the Halifax turned westwards on to its homeward heading, now considerably lighter and more manoeuvrable with the shedding of its four-ton bomb-load. Crew morale ran high with the prospect of a quick two-hour flight back to base and perhaps an early night. At approximately 0115 hours, just five minutes after departing from the target, the gunners alerted the crew by reporting their sightings of several aircraft going down in flames.

Almost immediately, without any indications of a night fighter being in the vicinity, a prolonged burst of heavy cannon fire shattered the port wing of the aircraft and both radial engines burst into flames and stopped. Sandy, our experienced pilot, immediately put the bomber into a violent evasive corkscrew manoeuvre – as the aircraft rapidly lost height, the whole port wing burst into flame as the petrol tanks were ruptured. The order to bail out was passed and acknowledged by each crew member in an orderly and disciplined manner.

Taffy, in his selfless and utterly professional manner, quickly jettisoned his trailing aerial (to avoid injuring any escaping parachutist) and struggled from his seat directly below the pilot and, regardless of his own personal safety, clambered into the cockpit to give what assistance he could to Sandy, who was battling with the controls of the shuddering and uncontrollable aircraft.

The navigator and bomb-aimer, down in the nose, cleared with difficulty the navigator's bench seat and folding plotting table which were blocking access to the main parachute hatch in the floor, this being the only exit for the pilot, wireless operator, bomb-aimer and navigator.

When the rapidly disintegrating bomber had dropped to approximately 4,000ft, a second burst of cannon fire shattered the starboard wing and at the same time riddled the cockpit with bullets, fatally wounding the two brave airmen, Sandy and Taffy, as they battled in vain to stabilize the aircraft in a level altitude thus enabling the members of the crew to make their escape as best they could.

The bomb-aimer and navigator had just struggled out through the open hatch in the floor as the Halifax went out of control and into a steep dive. As their parachutes opened, the aircraft was seen to crash, a mass of searing fire, a few miles further to the north.

Despite the thorough flying training given to all aircrew prior to joining an operational squadron, surprisingly little time was given to explaining and practising the operation of the parachute, and emergency drills were confined to regular 'abandon aircraft' and 'dinghy drills' in the airfield dispersal pans. No balloon or simulated parachute jumps had ever been undertaken and it came as quite a shock, other than for pilots with their backpacks, when on pulling the ripcord their chest packs flew over their heads, often causing severe facial abrasions, as the main parachute billowed out. So it proved for the navigator without the protection of the flying helmet which had been left behind in the aircraft . . .

ARTHUR DE BREYNE, RAF

Our final operation against the Cambrai marshalling yards on the night of 12 June [1944] provided more action than we had bargained for. With very little warning time we were engaged by a Ju88 from underneath. The rear gunner had observed a twin-engined aircraft below for a fleeting moment and lost him. I immediately initiated a corkscrew to starboard at 5,000ft. No sooner had I initiated the dive when three distinct explosions took place, two of which I could definitely locate in the port wing. At that point the conditions facing me had changed from day to night. I checked all engines for response and got none from the port side. Moreover we had sustained loss of intercom, and the instrument panel had turned black. I looked round for reference points on the horizon and the only one was a searchlight at 10 o'clock, ten miles off the port wing. I applied rudder and elected to keep it in that position to keep the port wing high at all times. I was tempted to turn towards it to use it as a rate-of-descent indicator but I might then have dropped the port wing – something I could not afford to do.

As we were probably down to 3,000ft I could see no way of this aircraft making it home and judged my first duty to bail out the crew while there was still time. I signalled with my hand to the flight engineer to get everyone out as fast as possible and signalled on the light a 'P' for the gunners, which lit up, and I knew the message was received.

My task now was to lose altitude as slowly as possible, keep the port wing high, as I could not afford to throttle back the starboard engines, yet avoid at all cost a stall. This was no easy feat: the searchlight told me how high my wing was, but nothing about my rate of descent. Another searchlight dead ahead would have been just fine, but it was not to be. I had to judge my speed by the sound of the wind and avoid moving the control column forward or backward unless I could definitely sense an acceleration or drop in speed. I was probably losing altitude faster than I should, but had no way of knowing.

To make matters worse, the bailing-out process stalled. More than a minute after giving the order, the navigator and wireless operator had not yet entered the bomb-aimer's compartment and I did not know why. I only got the answer to that one when I arrived back in London in September. The bomb-aimer had pulled up the hatch with a good tug and the rush of wind had blown it up against his head, knocking him out and leaving him with a sizeable cut above his eye, the scar of which he still carries. The flight engineer was faced with the task of clipping on his chute and dropping him through the hatch and following him out to release his chute and then his own. The navigator and wireless operator then disappeared in a flash.

And so did I, but not before throttling back both starboard engines to keep an even keel. I swung two or three times in the chute and within seconds was lying in a wheat field after a dead landing, but thankfully with my seat pack to cushion the landing as the ground had come up to meet me without any warning. I felt a great sense of satisfaction in having gotten all my crew out before the crash, which I listened for but did not hear, which puzzled me.

My next job was to get home and I had a distinct advantage over my comrades because I spoke French. After many adventures and some tremendous support from my French helpers I returned to England together, in September 1944, with three members of my crew. The bomb-aimer and the flight engineer were taken prisoner and my remaining member, Pilot Officer Andrew Mynarski, VC, lost his life in the vain attempt to save our rear gunner.

Later I found that when I throttled back the starboard engines to keep the aircraft on an even keel while I jumped, I also saved the life of my rear gunner, Flying Officer GP Brophy, without knowing it. As close as I can estimate, this occurred at about 700ft and had the effect of bringing up the nose of the aircraft gradually, so that when it reached the ground it was in a nearly perfect landing attitude. It seems that the port wing struck a large tree which tore it off, but must have slowed the speed of the fuselage considerably. We can only speculate on the details of Brophy being released from the turret. I have spoken to the man who picked him up and spirited him away, and he found it incredible he did not have a broken bone. Fortunately, the bombs did not explode but were scattered about in the field.

DOUGLAS CAMERON, RAF

On the night of 27–28 November 1942, our 149 Squadron Stirling took off with Flight Sergeant RH Middleton at the controls and headed for Turin, where our target was the Fiat Works. We got airborne as darkness was falling and had great difficulty climbing

with our full load of bombs and fuel. We had to reach 12,000ft
to clear the Alps, and this was only just achieved, leading to
excessive fuel consumption – which was to make its effect later
on. Middleton had to decide whether to continue, such was the
fuel consumption; however, we spotted flares ahead marking the
target, so pressed on.

Upon arriving over the target we dived to 2,000ft and made three
flights across the target to positively identify it. This burned more
precious fuel.

At 2200 hours we were hit by ferocious anti-aircraft fire. The first
hit blew a hole in the port main-plane, which made the aircraft very
unstable. Moments later a shell struck the cockpit and exploded,
shattering the windscreen, wounding both pilots, Middleton and
Hyder. Middleton lost an eye and it seemed half of his jaw and was
also wounded in the body and legs. Hyder and the wireless operator
were also quite badly wounded, but Hyder managed to keep the
aircraft flying as Middleton had lost consciousness. We were now
at 1,500ft, and managed to release our bombs.

We collected more and more hits from gunfire, meanwhile all
three gunners kept firing continuously; we left the target area with
a good fire burning in the Fiat Works.

Middleton regained consciousness and although critically
injured managed to get the aircraft back to the Kent coast where he
ordered his reluctant crew to bale out. Two refused and remained
with Middleton but sadly the aircraft came down in the sea and
all three were drowned. The whole crew were decorated, and
Middleton deservedly received the Victoria Cross posthumously.

Similar bravery earned the VC for a member of a Lancaster crew during
a raid on Schweinfurt.

NORMAN JACKSON, RAF

For the mission to Schweinfurt we were allocated a fresh Lancaster,

ME669, ZN-0. Taking off a few minutes after 0930, we set course southwards. While climbing out of the target area, after bombing, our aircraft was attacked by an enemy fighter. We were hit by a stream of bullets and a fire started in No 1 starboard petrol tank. During the attack I was thrown to the floor with shrapnel wounds to the right leg and shoulder. I reckoned, with luck, I could put the fire out; I pushed a hand fire extinguisher into the top of my life jacket, clipped on my parachute pack, and jettisoned the escape hatch above the pilot's seat, but before I could climb out my parachute opened and the whole canopy and rigging lines spilled into the cockpit. I ignored this and continued my journey. The pilot, bomb-aimer and navigator gathered the parachute and held on to the rigging lines – paying them out as I climbed out. I lowered my feet onto the starboard wing and flung myself forward and down into the airstream and grasped at the air intake on the leading edge of the wing.

Tightening the group with my left hand, holding the extinguisher with my right, I pressed the nozzle into the exhaust entry of No 1 engine. After a couple of seconds the fire died down and then stopped. Suddenly the aircraft lurched to the left, and I realized that the fight had found us again.

I felt stabbing pains in my back, the engine exploded into flames and I slipped off the wing. A violent jerk told me I was still attached to the Lancaster by my parachute. I was being pulled downwards in a spiralling arc. The other crew members paid out the rest of my canopy before bailing out themselves. I was unable to control the descent of my slashed and torn parachute, and I landed heavily in a forest. After regaining consciousness I checked my injuries. Both ankles seemed broken, my legs and back ached from shell splinters and shrapnel; both my hands and face were severely burned and my right eye was completely closed up.

At daybreak I managed to crawl to a nearby cottage, but was welcomed by a tirade of insults; 'Churchill gangster!' 'Terror

Flieger.' After being paraded through town for more jeers I joined my fellow crew members – happily all intact – for a 12-hour journey to Dulag Laft. Crippled and temporarily blind, I spent 10 months in a German hospital before being moved to a POW Camp, where I saw out the war.

As always, the other side was sharing the risks and the terror of combat, including the prospect of bailing out.

MARTIN DREWES, LUFTWAFFE

On 3 October 1943, I attacked a group of low-flying Short Stirling bombers near the burning town of Kassel but, silhouetted by the blood-red sky, could not approach unseen. When I opened fire, I was immediately bombarded by two bombers from behind and below, which I hadn't seen. With my right wing burning and a wound to my head, I lost height. I ordered my crew to jump but, weakening, I had left it too late to get out myself. Switching on my spotlights, I lined up for an emergency landing when a tree appeared in front of me. Pulling the stick into my stomach, my Me110G momentarily came under control before ploughing into the slopes of the Allendorf Mountain at 250mph and tearing uphill into an orchard, pulling several trees out of the ground. When the aircraft came to rest, I freed myself and ran clear, throwing myself to the ground a short distance away before the ammunition exploded in all directions. Miraculously, I had survived.

On another night, I came equally close to death over Lake Zuider when pressing home an attack on a Lancaster at about 20,000ft. The aircraft, approaching from the right, flew right over the top of me, hardly 50m away. Aiming between the two port engines at no more than 30m distance, I opened fire with my upwards-firing guns. In a flash, everything turned into a ball of fire. I had hit the bomb bay. My aircraft plunged downwards and with my eyes swollen shut and in great pain, I managed to bail out. When I pulled the parachute handle, I swung just twice before hitting the ground. My crew landed close by, with my gunner's watch, hit by a splinter, having stopped at 0119 hours. It was several months before I could fly again at night.

Sometimes valuable lessons could be learned from near-disaster, as in this instance:

MICK MARTIN, RAF

Probably the most memorable operational sortie in which I ever took part was an attack on Kassel. Whilst over the target our aircraft struck a steel cable held aloft by a barrage balloon. The cable snapped from both the balloon's anchorage above and the winch which attached it to the ground and draped itself around the port wing and trailed out of sight. Shortly afterwards a night fighter attacked us and we quickly took evasive action by diving. One end of the cable caught itself on something on the ground and (Lady Luck must have been smiling on us that day!) the rest of that potentially lethal hawser unwound itself from around the wing and fell free from our aircraft, but in so doing tore into the leading edge and main spar.

Later, more accurate analysis of the cut by specialists at base revealed the essential information that the diameter of the cable at the top had been much thicker than the anchorage end on the winch at the bottom, which was therefore considerably weaker. A useful and potentially life-saving conclusion was evident: if caught in a balloon barrage we would be well advised to fly as low and as fast as we possibly could. From then on the policy of flying below the heavy ack-ack bursts, down where balloon cables were weakest and night fighters' radar effectiveness poor, was to be a dominant feature of our tactics in such situations for the duration of hostilities.

To the defending fighter pilots the sight of American bomber formations must have been overwhelming, even though they knew that they were able to tear gaping holes in them:

PAUL ZORNER, LUFTWAFFE

On 25 July 1943, at around 2330 hours, I was ordered up to intercept a force of bombers flying over the German Bight. Despite a height advantage of nearly 2,000ft the thought that I now had to pursue them with the Northern Lights behind me made me uncomfortable. I [therefore] maintained my altitude until I was about 500m behind a single bomber, a Halifax, going into a steep glide until I was about 1,000 feet below him . . .

I let fly a burst of fire which set the bomber burning and it fell away in a right-hand spiral, crashing in a huge inferno. I then headed for home, but two minutes later felt a bang from my right engine, which burst into flames. The left engine couldn't cope on its own and we gradually lost height. Despite getting the runway lights into view, we had to take to our parachutes.

This had been a typical night's combat and illustrated how weather conditions and visibility had to be taken into account when deciding how best to approach enemy aircraft before attacking. In my 59 night victories I only received return fire on six occasions.

The development of long-range fighter escort was the greatest single improvement in the lives of those who flew the bombers. A fighter pilot remembered:

DANNY BROWNE, RCAF

During the summer [of 1943] we escorted the first Fortress raids into combat. They took some very hard knocks and it was not until the most significant fighter of the war came along, the North American Mustang, that the 8th Air Force was able to fly to Berlin and back without undue losses.

When the American long-range fighters came into the theatre it changed the character of the air war; the German fighter squadrons were pulled back from the coast and operated from bases nearer the centre of Germany where the bombing targets were located.

This caused a shift of emphasis for our squadrons to ground attack operations, especially because of the forthcoming invasions of Europe. Ground attack does not have the romance of the air duels, but in the later stages of the war the fighter-bombers of the Royal Air Force and the US Army Air Force were the cutting edge of the Allied armies that swept on to victory.

In the autumn of 1944, Bomber Command was again in pursuit of the German battleship *Tirpitz*, flying once more to Norway. The leader of the raid recalled:

JAMES TAIT, RAF

Moored in Alten Fjord, in the Arctic Circle by the northern tip of Norway, the *Tirpitz* simply by being there had forced the Allies to divert three battleships, badly needed elsewhere.

Because the *Tirpitz* was out of range of Lossiemouth, the aircrafts' Scottish base, they had to fly to Russia and begin the mission from there:

On 15 September the weather cleared and 28 Lancasters took off. As I led in over Alten Fjord at 11,100ft, the German defensive smokescreen was already beginning to shroud the *Tirpitz*. In the nose of my Lancaster my bomb aimer [Danny] Daniel had taken a long bead on the *Tirpitz*, but by the time he got his bomb away she was enveloped in smoke. The following aircraft all bombed blind.

One of the other bomb-aimers was sure he had seen Daniel's tallboy hit the target but it was days before it was confirmed. The damaged battleship was moved south to Tromsö Fjord, possibly for repair, which brought her just within range of Lossiemouth.

After several false starts, on 12 November I led 617 Squadron, again with 9 Squadron, and headed for Tromsö. This time there was no cloud, no smoke and no enemy fighters. All 31 aircraft dropped their bombs, and when they departed the *Tirpitz* had taken on a noticeable list. Shortly after she rolled over and sank.

His bomb-aimer also provided memories of the missions:

DANNY DANIEL, RCAF

We took off on 15 September 1944, and approached the target from a direction that surprised the enemy, thus giving us a short advantage. Tait turned our Lancaster on to the bombing run and made a superb run over the target, allowing me to get the battleship beautifully into the cross[-hairs] of my bomb sights. Just before I released the six-ton bomb, the ship was lost in the smokescreen. However, as we completed our run I saw a terrific explosion, indicating that we had scored a direct hit. Intelligence reports later told us that we had damaged the *Tirpitz* so badly that she had to go back to Germany for repairs.

[After a further unsuccessful attempt to destroy her on] 9 October, we managed to sink the *Tirpitz* on the raid of 12 November.

Flying the fast and versatile Mosquito, Group Captain Leonard Cheshire led an attack on Munich which used a new technique. The C-in-C had agreed that he could have his Mosquitos if he could mark Munich successfully. If not, they would be taken back.

LEONARD CHESHIRE, RAF

On arrival at Munich, [we were] quickly coned by German searchlights. At Zero minus five, as I was approaching the western suburbs at 8,000ft the flares ignited, and by the time I had orientated myself the aiming point – the Gestapo headquarters – lay immediately under my port wing. Normally this would have forced me to fly on a mile or so in order to dive-bomb at an angle of 45 degrees, but because of shortage of fuel and my anxiety not to lose sight of the aiming point, I dropped the wing and put the aircraft into a vertical dive. The problem in this, apart from the fact that we were well exceeding the safety speed limit, is that if you release the bombs in a vertical position they fall through the forward bulkhead and destroy the aircraft. On the other hand, if you pull the nose up even marginally before releasing the bombs they are likely to be thrown off target; the two movements have to be done simultaneously. By the grace of God this happened and we achieved an accurate mark, flattening out at some 700ft and climbing steeply back to 6,000. At that moment there were lights on the ground, flares above and flak on all sides, and it was a little difficult to know whether we were upside down or what. However, the incomparable Mossie has a habit of sorting things out herself if left to it, and it all ended well.

Reconnaissance reports showed that [the raid on] Munich had been a complete success.

In the war's final months, as the Allied armies pushed steadily eastward across Europe, there was no let-up in the risks that faced bomber pilots. This account suggests that new developments in both weaponry and parachutes had made the air war more sophisticated, although no less dangerous:

JOHN COSTELLO, RAF

On 21 February 1945, we attacked the Mitteland Canal at Gravenhorst from a height of 6–8,000ft and attained one of the densest concentrations of bombing yet seen, the canal being completely drained. It was the second night running on this target and on the way home we were shot down by a fighter using an upward-firing cannon. Both our inboard engines were set ablaze and we were ordered to abandon the aircraft some ten minutes

flying time from Allied Lines. Five out of the eight crew escaped
by parachute and I was the last man out through the front hatch. I
made a safe but bumpy landing using a new type back-chute which
I had volunteered to test. It worked!

While the RAF flew its missions at night, the daytime skies belonged to
the US Army Air Force. The American bomber fleets flew at high altitude
– usually 22,000ft – and this meant operating in a sub-zero world where
equipment froze, frostbite could be as threatening as enemy tracer, and
multiple layers of clothing, including electrically-heated flight-suits, had
to be worn.

Though more heavily armed than a Lancaster, a B-17 – which had
ten machine guns as opposed to six – was equally vulnerable to flak and
fighters. Missions required as great a level of sustained courage, and
losses were almost as heavy (the USAAF lost 46,000 men, RAF Bomber
Command 55,000). Perceived as less glamourous than fighter pilots, these
men included in their ranks three names that were – or would be – well-
known in Hollywood: James Stewart, Clark Gable and Walter Mathau all
served with honour in the USAAF's bomber offensive.

An American crew would have spent two years, learning to fly and
bomb, at locations all over the United States before arriving in England.
Once in the ETO (European Theatre of Operations) they would face
the prospect of surviving 25 – later extended to 35 – missions before
completing their tour and becoming eligible to go home. This was a very
daunting prospect indeed, even for men who, like their counterparts in
the RAF, were schooled to a peak of competence and professionalism.

DONALD H SMITH, USAAF

Prior to about 1944 the standard tour of duty was 25 combat
missions. The Luftwaffe was much stronger in the early days of
the war . . . in those early tours crews had only one chance in three
of completing. Those who made it through were automatically
awarded the DFC. [Later] the tour was lengthened to 35 missions

and the DFC was no longer automatic. The Air Medal was given for each six missions. No ceremony.

I recall being outside one day when one of our enlisted men called to me: 'Hey Lieutenant, you got another Air Medal. I left it on your bunk.'

On days we didn't fly combat missions, we often flew practice missions, to give newer crews some formation flying experience.

Acclimatizing to conditions in England was often difficult, especially because a crew-member's fitness to fly depended so much on health.

DR ACKERSON, USAAF

Life was pretty hard. The Quonset hut was cold, no insulation at all, and the coal stove was in the middle so the beds nearest [it] were warm and everyone else was cold. Charcoal, coal and coke were all rationed and we never had enough. The latrine was a walk away and we got a hot shower about once a week. Meals were mass-produced K-rations and were pretty bad.

On the mornings when we flew, we had fresh eggs for breakfast and candy bars to eat while we were in the air. Since we usually flew at 22,000ft and the planes were not pressurized, we had to watch our diet. Gas-producing foods like beans, cabbage, etc, could give you real problems on a flight. We all got colds at one time or another because of the English winter weather . . . and flying with a cold could be very bad. You had to clear your ears when going up or down because of the lack of pressurization of the planes. This meant that you could break your eardrums if you came down too fast and couldn't clear your ears. I was grounded once with a very bad cold.

When setting out on a mission, the first anxiety was learning of the target. This was introduced at a morning briefing. A notoriously well-defended city could send spirits plummeting:

BILL ETHERIDGE, USAAF

> The bullschmere [inflated tone] made it pretty obvious that we were
> not going on any milk run, and when the curtains were pulled back
> to reveal the 'Target for Today' a wave of groans and cuss-words
> flooded the room. We were headed for Berlin, the 'Big B'. We had
> listened to other crews' horror stories about the concentration of
> both flak and fighters protecting the city . . .

The plane assigned to a crew, or their seniority within a unit, could
significantly affect their chances of survival. The same pilot recalled that:

> Veteran crews (approaching their 35th mission) were given the best
> planes available, to increase their chances of getting through.
> Because we were the newest crew . . . we flew 'tail-end charlie',
> a position that the German fighters just loved. Charlie was the last
> plane in the Squadron with no one protecting his tail.

When airborne, the hazards began at once, with the problem of
manoeuvring huge numbers of aircraft into formation.

> The amount of air traffic in and out of the [Suffolk air-] fields
> was tremendous and when combined with the frequent English
> fog, even the most skilled pilots needed a bit of luck to avoid
> collisions. While accidents did happen, they were comparatively
> few considering the archaic navigational equipment and traffic-
> control procedures.

DR ACKERSON, USAAF

> [Our Group] had a mid-air collision on the assembly and lost two
> ships and two crews.

At their customary high altitude, the health of the bomber crews began to
suffer in the freezing temperatures.

DR ACKERSON USAAF

When we flew out of England it was almost always –50F outside at our usual altitude of 20–22,000ft . . . Jesse Pond froze his hands on our first mission and most of us had a touch of frostbite at one time or another. All of this was in a non-pressurized plane with open windows in the radio and both waist-gunner positions.

The heated equipment was always going out, so we wore it under our fleece-lined heavy flying-suits. Long-johns, three pairs of socks, wool pants and shirts, sweaters, etc, kept us fairly comfortable except in the waist [gun positions]. Our gunnery was good despite the incredible passing speed of a small enemy fighter. We rarely had a gun failure and engine failures were fairly rare. Quite a few times we went on to the target with an engine giving us trouble but it never turned out to be serious . . .

En route to the target a series of drills had to be gone through. The flight engineer would have each gunner fire a short burst to check the functioning of his weapons, and breathing apparatus would also be tested.

DR ACKERSON USAAF

We were a well-trained crew and everyone knew their jobs. We had oxygen checks at regular intervals and everyone had to report in, in order, on the command 'Oxygen Check!' This made sure that no one passed out and didn't get noticed.

Flying with a westerly wind behind them, planes could reach their objective more quickly than they could return from it.

DONALD H SMITH, USAAF

B-17 standard airspeed was 150mph. In thin air at high altitude, 150mph equalled 250mph groundspeed. In a jetstream tailwind one day we went over the target at 420mph groundspeed – 12 minutes from the coast to Hamburg, over an hour back to the coast.

ROBERT S JOHNSON, USAAF

We made our rendezvous with the bombers near the Zuider Zee at 25,000ft and split into finger-fours and positioned ourselves several thousand feet out from our big friends. We had to make continual 'S' turns to stay with the slower bombers. Near the German border, Mike Quirk's eight P-47s broke hard right. They jumped some Me109s and had quite a battle, but he would not give us his location. Maybe they wanted all the Huns for themselves!

We flew over the Dummer Lake – an unmistakeable landmark – and the three boxes of bombers we escorted flew silently and majestically on – dozens of forts in each close-packed box.

Once over continental Europe, trouble was often quick in coming.

BILL ETHERIDGE, USAAF

The Germans had learned to attack shortly after our fighters crossed the English Channel. Our escorts would then drop their fuel tanks in order to dogfight. After the drop-tanks had been jettisoned, the Germans would leave, thereby denying the bombers air cover over the target area and for part of the return trip back to England. About all our fighters could do was to return to England, refuel, and meet us returning from our targets. The Allies finally countered this by sending up more fighters.

Arming the bombs was necessary as the target drew nearer.

DONALD H SMITH, USAAF

During our climb to formation altitude . . . Lieutenant Scott went into the bomb bay and took the pins out of the bombs. (Each bomb carried a small propeller on its nose. This was secured by a pin for safety in ground handling and loading. With the pin removed the bomb was armed and would explode on impact.) A normal load was 12,500lb bombs or 61,000 pounders.

DONALD F MUNDELL, USAAF

Nearing the target the bombardier opened the bomb bay doors in preparation for the bomb run, and since the bomb doors on a B-24 tended to creep shut once they were opened, it was the duty of the radio operator to go down to the bomb bay and push an 'anti-creep' lever to hold the doors open. I went down to the bomb bay, pushed the lever, and waited for the release of the bombs . . .

However, any aircraft could suffer mechanical failure of some sort, causing a crew to have to abandon the mission even before reaching the target, or even to bail out and face captivity, and once enemy fighters appeared an aircraft's fate could be quickly sealed:

DR ACKERSON, USAAF

Somewhere in the Luxembourg area, we had our first fighter attacks on the lead group. They were about 20 Me109s . . . A few minutes later we were hit by about 30 FW-190s who made a pass from 12 and 11 o'clock almost level. Our ship was hit on that first pass and number 3 engine caught fire. The engine was feathered at once but the fire spread through the wing and into the bomb bay, melting the bulkhead away. The radio-operator informed the pilot and he gave the order to bail out. The navigator, after making sure that I had heard the order, bailed out followed by the engineer. I was behind the engineer as the bombs were still in and I was trying to get them out.

I left immediately after the bombs were away. I pulled a partially delayed jump, delaying for a few thousand feet. Lost consciousness from the lack of oxygen or the jerk of the 'chute opening, and came to at about 18,000ft and watched our P-51 escort, which was late that day, circle around me. I floated quietly down. It took about 16 minutes. I had a good landing – in a ploughed field with a farmer shooting at me with a rifle while I was coming down. I could see Home Guard soldiers running up the road and they took me into custody, kicking me because I said 'Nein' when they said 'For you the war is over'.

DONALD H SMITH, USAAF

Perhaps four hours after take-off, at circa 25,000ft (assigned altitude), black oil was spewing out of the top of the right inboard engine nacelle . . . flames appeared through the cowling. Fortunately the Co^2 fire-extinguisher worked. Meanwhile, we had to drop out of formation, staying clear of other ships. Then old 222 began to shake. With no oil, the pistons, driven by the windmilling prop, were red-hot and trying to freeze in the cylinders, but the torque of the prop was too strong. The shakings became so violent that pieces were hitting the prop, which was throwing them against the fuselage. I expected the wings to be shaken off.

Gridley activated the alarm bell, in a series of short rings, the signal for the crew to prepare to bail out. The violent shaking continued. We could hardly hold on to the wheel. He looked at me: 'Shall we go?' I suppose my dread of a German prison camp outweighed my better judgement. I remember replying: 'Not yet. It's still flying.' Suddenly there was a terrific jolt, then the shaking stopped. The propeller shaft had broken loose inside what was left of the engine, and the prop was windmilling freely.

Eventually Gridley returned to his seat, commenced chain-smoking, gave orders for the crew to throw out everything that would come loose, to lighten our load. Out went oxygen bottles, flak suits, etc. He even dropped our 14.50 calibre machine guns and the ball-turret. As soon as Art (the navigator) got us located, which took some time, we dropped the bombs 'safe' (eg, re-armed, with the pins back in) into a small wooded area in France.

Less crucial, but distinctly unpleasant for those affected, were the human problems suffered by men obliged to spend long hours in a cramped and bucking aircraft.

DONALD H SMITH, USAAF

Frank Jones . . . had been airsick on practically every flight throughout his training. He had flown perhaps 20 combat missions. Same thing. He routinely carried two rubberized bags to meet his needs . . .

. . . there was the day Cal Mattson, the ball-turret gunner, had diarrhoea. He had to fly anyway. Before he got into his turret he relieved himself in some leaky box he found in the radio room. Down in his turret he had no choice but to let go, inside his flying-suit, all day. I knew Cal was having problems, but had no idea of the magnitude until we cut the engines back in the revetment, and the atmosphere from the rear of the plane drifted forward. Then we knew.

By this stage in a mission enemy flak would be bursting around each plane.

BILL ETHERIDGE, USAAF

[Flak was] dreaded more than the fighters. Fighters we could see, but until they exploded, the flak-bursts were impossible to anticipate. And we couldn't return the fire.

The flak first appeared as ink-black clouds with hellish-red centres; at one point a black puff appeared directly in front of the plane, giving us an experience somewhat like driving too close behind a gravel truck that was spilling its contents on to the roadway.

I must have jumped a foot when a piece of shrapnel broke through the nose and hit the bulkhead directly behind me. A searing pain knifed across the back of my neck and I could feel a trickle of blood between my leather helmet and coat collar.

The sky turned a deathly black as two shells exploded directly in front of us. Evasive action was out of the question and so the pilots opted to fly directly through the cloud and hope for the best.

DONALD F MUNDELL, USAAF

Looking down through the open [bomb] doors at the flak exploding below us, I wondered how we were going to get through it all. Flak looks like harmless grey puffs of smoke when seen from a distance, but it's actually a huge grenade hurling large pieces of shrapnel.

Even at this late stage, a mission could be cancelled owing to weather conditions. Once launched, it was extremely difficult to turn around one of the huge bomber fleets and return it to base.

DONALD H SMITH, USAAF

We were in the usual column of groups. Groups were separated by two or three minutes. A group did not fly directly behind the one ahead. Prop-wash was too violent. Far over Germany, the mission was recalled (possibly due to deteriorating weather conditions back over England). Each group was to do a 180-degree turn to the left. Our group awaited its turn. The group behind us, offset to our left to avoid our prop-wash, did not hear the recall order. They continued to fly straight ahead. Suddenly that group flew right through ours . . . amazingly there were no mid-air collisions, but 80 planes were scattered all over the German sky.

Assuming all went well, and with the target almost below them, pilots would look for the markers dropped by the lead plane.

DONALD H SMITH, USAAF

The group leader and his deputy carried smoke markers. The lead bombardier tracked the target either by radar or by using his Norden bombsight. When his bombs were dropped, the white smoke markers went first and all other bombardiers 'toggled' on the leader. This presumably gave a good, compact pattern on the ground.

The danger was increasing. Enemy planes would be weaving in and out of the formations. The sky would be filled with machine gun fire as well as flak. Planes would be burning . . .

DR ACKERSON, USAAF

Our group had no trouble until we neared the target. A group in front was really getting pasted by about ten FW-190s. We saw three B-17s go down in flames. Then more than 20 FW-190s lined up and came in low from 11 o'clock. Just as they came near, our P-38 escort jumped them and they scattered. Our escort really saved our skins that day . . .

ROBERT S JOHNSON, USAAF

Suddenly, gaggles of FW-190s attacked the bombers head-on. We were so close to our big friends that we had no hope of stopping the 190s who ignored us and went straight for the bombers.

American and German fighters flashed together at over 600mph. In a second, they were past us. We followed them into the bomber formations whose gunners fired at friend and foe alike. Enemy 20mm shells threw white bursts into the bombers and rockets left zigzag trails as they struck the heavies.

The March air was filled with cries of warning and combat. One B-17 was cut in half and I thought 'a few seconds ago those ten men were safe and sound'. Others dropped out of the lead box, trailing smoke, crippled. Several plunged earthwards, trailing black columns of smoke. A hundred parachutes filled the sky.

During that desperate, fierce fighting we did our best to protect our big friends and although my pilots shot down several enemy fighters the Eighth lost 69 bombers (690 men) on this first major day of daylight bombing of Berlin.

BILL ETHERIDGE, USAAF

I was mesmerized by what was happening; both sides were taking losses, parachutes were popping everywhere and . . . I found myself urging our guys on and on until Sobolof punched me in the left rib-cage and pointed to the upcoming checkpoint. I quickly got with it, checking my calculations, twisting the knobs on the bomb-sight, and so on down the mental checklist.

As we crossed our checkpoint . . . I took over flying via the auto-pilot. The pilot's job was then to keep the plane at the prescribed altitude and speed so that with the auto-pilot and bomb-sight locked together I could direct the plane to the exact position to release the bombs, all the while praying for a stable platform. At this altitude a 12-inch lift to our wing-tip could throw any bomb-drop several hundred feet off to one side and beyond the target. Between the turbulent air from the cumulus clouds and the exploding anti-aircraft shells, the pilots and I struggled to achieve the desirable platform.

My Norden sight was right on as it clicked the instant I tripped the manual switch on the count of three following the lead [aircraft]. As soon as our bombs cleared the bomb-bay I quickly closed the door to reduce the drag and as I did so I could feel the plane edge forward.

Even as the bomb-load was released disaster could strike.

BILL ETHERIDGE, USAAF

Synchronizing was easy, and the cross-hairs were staying on our assigned target. Just prior to dropping I could see bombs from the far lead plane strike the first building in the complex, followed by others just a little further in. When my sight released I knew we would score a direct hit as well. The cross-hairs had moved with the plane and they had stayed right on! The pilot had done a wonderful job of maintaining a constant speed and my auto-pilot had kept it straight and level.

. . . immediately after 'bombs away' the engineer had called in a panic: 'We have a hung bomb!' With my own panic button flashing I grabbed my tool-kit, took out a long-handled screwdriver, disconnected my oxygen line and was in the bomb-bay in about five seconds flat. We were safe from an explosion providing we did not take a hit in the bomb-bays from fighters or anti-aircraft. I had pried dummy bombs loose while on the ground, but this was no drill and everything was frozen . . .

And it might turn out that the target had been missed altogether in the confusion.

DONALD H SMITH, USAAF

We came from the south. As we opened our bomb-bay doors, on order from the group leader, the deputy-leader's smoke-marker accidentally went away. All bombardiers except the lead bombardier were to release their bombs by toggle switch. They mistook the deputy's smoke-marker for the leader's, and the entire formation dropped their bombs, 40 to 50 miles short of the target. The only plane still carrying bombs was the leader's. He took the entire formation through the Augsburg anti-aircraft fire, so he could drop his bombs on target. Flak was quite light, and we did not lose any planes in that fiasco.

Once the bombs were gone, there was often a sense of euphoria that the job was done. The signs that bombs had hit their target – explosions or smoke – could create a feeling of achievement among those who had put their lives at such risk to reach it. It was this, and not any desire for destruction, that could prompt a semblance of pleasure among crews.

DONALD H SMITH, USAAF

The sight of black oil-smoke boiling up through the clouds after we had bombed the port of Hamburg brought grins to our faces . . .

Some crew members experienced more than just euphoria:

DONALD H SMITH, USAAF

After the bomb run one day: 'Navigator to pilot.'

'Yes, Art.'

'I pissed my pants on that one.'

'We've got an extra pair on the flight deck. Come get it.'

A short time later, from Art: 'I did it again.'

This wasn't so funny at the time. Temperature at high altitude could be minus 50 degrees, and the suits were electrically heated. We worried about short circuits. Somehow Art made it back to base with essential organs intact . . .

The plane was now lighter, and faster. If left alone by fighters, its crew could start to think about returning home.

DONALD H SMITH, USAAF

This late in the war the capabilities of the German Luftwaffe had been greatly diminished, and their fuel was short. Their strategy was to pick an isolated plane, squadron or group and make a single pass, perhaps 20 planes abreast, through the bomber formation, blasting with their machine guns as they went. I was on the radio, Cliff on the intercom. Suddenly I heard almost a scream: 'Green Low has bandits on its tail!' As I switched to the other channel to tell our crew, I found out that they already knew. Our own 50-calibre machine guns began to chatter, and I could see several ts streak through our formation, travelling at least 100mph faster than we were moving. Two waves hit us, then silence.

I shall always remember the pang of fear that hit me when I realized we were under fighter attack, then the remarkable calm I felt as I waited for the hot lead to come through the back of my seat – and through me. Then relief as we appeared to be intact.

As we assessed the damage, we learned our waist-gunner had a sliver in his forearm from an exploding shell, and the plane had minor damage on one wing. Our flight engineer, who manned the upper turret, was excited. His adrenaline was pumping. He was sure he had gotten one of the attacking planes. (He was credited with a 'probable').

DONALD F MUNDELL, USAAF

We dropped our bombs on the target, closed the bomb-bay doors, and headed back, thinking the tough part was over. Whitlock even asked me if I could find some music on the radio. About that time someone said over the intercom that he had spotted some German fighters. Another voice said, 'Looks like they're coming in.' I looked back and caught a glimpse of some fighters behind us and to our left. They were headed our way.

A wave of them came in and raked us pretty good. But we were still flying, and I thought they might leave. But that was not to be. There was only one burst from our tail gunner; apparently he was killed on that first pass. That left our tail wide open, and we didn't have fighter escort.

They came in again, plenty of them, and shot the plane up badly. There were bullets buzzing all over the place. There wasn't much for a radio operator to do during an attack, so I stood directly behind the pilots and watched the fight from their vantage-point . . .

Within minutes, however, he was as busy as the rest of the crew.

A big fire had broken out in the bomb-bay, and I emptied a big fire-extinguisher at it. It had no effect on the fire. When I returned to the flight deck, Whitlock said it was time to get out, that he was losing control of the plane.

This could be easier said than done, as Mundell discovered.

There were normally two exits available to the four of us on the flight deck. One was to drop out of the bottom of the plane through the bomb-bay, the other was to use the top hatch. The top hatch was not a good way to exit a B-24 in flight. Immediately behind it was the top turret, and further back along the top of the fuselage were some antennas. When exiting an aeroplane in flight – especially one going as fast as we were – the wind-stream hurled you back toward the tail. If you cleared the top turret and the antennas, you could still strike the tail. We were told in training to drop out through the bomb-bay, but that was no longer an option – the bomb-bay was now engulfed in flames.

The top hatch was already open. I reached [it] and was halfway out when I got hung up. The top half of me was outside the plane, and the blast from the ice-cold wind was numbing. The wind had caught my belly pack [parachute] and it was now floating four feet from me. The straps felt like they were going to pull through me. I was praying the chute wouldn't open before I got clear of the plane. I kept struggling, but I could feel my strength ebbing. Then I felt a hand push me.

Whitlock had reached up and given me a shove. It was enough to free me, and out I went. I hit something that skinned my knee, and . . . the next thing I knew my chute was open . . .

Mundell was captured, on reaching the ground, near the spot where his plane came down. He and his captors passed the wreckage moments later.

We continued for another quarter of a mile and came upon the body of Emil Kosch, one of the waist-gunners. A hundred yards beyond lay the wreckage of our B-24. Kosch's legs had been shot up but his body, though contorted, was intact. I don't know if he had been on the plane when it hit the ground – it didn't seem like he could have been thrown that far – or if he had fallen from the plane. [The aircraft] was still burning. The skeleton of the gunner was still in the tail turret; the fire had burned away most of the flesh. Some of the more morbid of our captors took great delight in taunting us and pointing to the badly-charred remains.

Fortunately, other crew members had survived.

> A little later they brought in Ricks (navigator) and Waite
> (bombardier), who had dropped out through the nose-wheel doors.
> Ricks had seen Knox (well gunner) who had been injured. Bonham
> (tail gunner) and Kosch (waist gunner) had been killed in the attack.
> Dunajecz (waist-gunner) had died when his chute didn't open.
> Wilson (co-pilot) had burned to death trying to get out through the
> bomb-bay and Stewart (engineer) had remained on the plane all the
> way to the ground. We had lost five of our ten-man crew.

Other crews, limping home across Europe in heavily-damaged planes, had to prepare to ditch either over enemy territory or – what was worse – over the sea.

DONALD H SMITH, USAAF

> We were told that the North Sea was so cold that anyone
> parachuting into it had a 20-minute life-expectancy. On our return
> one day, in formation over the North Sea, a B-17 slid across in front
> of us, a short distance ahead. We could see crew members bailing
> out. They had virtually no chance of survival.

The tension of nursing a crippled aircraft and wondering if it would last as far as the English coast could be the most nerve-racking part of a mission.

BILL ETHERIDGE, USAAF

> During the return flight Sobolof and I noticed a decided droop to
> the right wing and I so notified Mateyka. [He] called every station on
> board and told them to make certain their parachutes were on and to
> stand by an exit prepared to jump should the wing start to give way.
> [Every] crew member remained on edge as we crossed

Holland. We were constantly scanning the sky for friendly or unfriendly aircraft. [Our] tanks were leaking from multiple ruptures caused by the heavy anti-aircraft explosions and the chances were slim that we would reach England or even the east coast of Holland. If we could gain only a few miles it might be the difference [between] landing in Holland or ditching away from the enemy-held coast. Anything having significant weight must go overboard! We removed and tossed all guns and ammunition except those in the ball- and chin-turret. Oxygen cylinders, flak-vests, hand-held fire-extinguishers and so on went out. The effects were noticed immediately as the plane ceased to lose altitude.

By now we could see the North Sea and within a minute or two Sobolof and I would need to give the pilots a recommended heading to exit the coast. A message [came] from the pilots: 'Our fuel tanks all show empty. Prepare to ditch.'

Wind squalls were skimming the tops of the waves and slinging water several feet beyond their crests . . . the instructions on ditching cautioned crews to exit the aircraft as quickly as possible, then rapidly move away from the aircraft before it sank and sucked everyone down with it. Estimates on the time a '17 would float ranged from one to five minutes. The instructions were repeated as we positioned ourselves backs-to-bellies, bobsled fashion, with all backs towards the forward bulkhead and our hands interlocked behind our heads.

We exited one by one via the top hatch as soon as we hit the water. The exiting was orderly and surprisingly unhurried. The pilots had popped the side hatches after hitting the water, and a ten-man rubber raft was waiting on each wing. At that moment, no one had to convince us that God was our co-pilot.

To our amazement, the B-17 stayed afloat for almost an hour. I will always believe this was due to empty fuel tanks and the ball-turret we did not drop over Holland.

Brian Kingcome in the cockpit with other pilots of 92 Squadron. (p163) Pilots on both sides kept detailed records of their successes, both individual and collective; intense competitiveness boosted morale and was an important aspect of the air war.

New Zealand ace Alan Deere (far right) discussing an operation with (from left) South African Group Captain 'Sailor' Malan, Squadron Leader Torre and Squadron Leader Jack Charles. (p46) While the Luftwaffe was strictly German, RAF Fighter Command was multi-national. Pilots came from all over the Commonwealth, from the United States and from countries overrun by the Nazis.

The Luftwaffe's most legendary – though not its highest-scoring – pilot. Adolf Galland's flamboyance in and out of the air made him as glamorous a figure as Douglas Bader, though his blunt criticism of the Nazi High Command made him unpopular with Hiter's circle. Nevertheless, he ended the war as a Generalleutenant (p172).

Leading German ace Erich Hartmann flew 1,400 missions in two and half years during the war, claiming 352 victories (pp155–158). He was never wounded, but after the war spent more than 10 years in Russian captivity. He survived the ordeal to become a senior officer in Germany's new air force.

Hannes Trautloft (p152), a Spanish Civil War veteran, he commanded units on both fronts in the 1939–45 conflict and also fought in the Balkans. The 'Green Heart' symbol on his fuselage was a sentimental reference to his home-region: Thuringia, the heart of Germany.

Eduard Neumann, (pp56–57) another Spanish veteran, he saw service in the Battle of Britain, the Balkans, North Africa and Italy, ending the war with 11 victories. Throughout the conflict he flew only one type of aircraft in combat: the Me109.

Johannes Steinhoff (p142) fought in Europe, North Africa and Russia. While piloting an Me262 at the end of the war he was badly disfigured in a crash, but went on to become a general in an air force career that lasted another three decades.

James Tait with members of the Lancaster crews that sank the German battleship *Tirpitz*. A vastly experienced and able bomber pilot, Tait led his force of Lancasters on their highly dangerous mission to Norway not once, but twice (15 September and 12 November 1944) damaging – and finally destroying – the great ship (p101).

Marion Carl, a US Marine, shot down 18 Japanese planes at Midway and in other battles (pp204–205). He was awarded the Navy Cross (twice), the DFC and the Legion of Merit (four times). After the war, he showed courage of a different sort as a test pilot.

Robert Johnson, who flew escort missions for the American bomber fleet over Germany, was the first US pilot to match Richenbacker's World War I record of 26 victories. His final tally was 27 (p108).

Robin Olds flew 107 combat missions for the US Army Air Corps from May 1944 until the end of the war. His score was 13 aircraft shot down and another 11 destroyed on the ground. A long post-war career in the USAAF included service in Vietnam and postings in England as commander of RAF units (p180).

Bob Stanford-Tuck in his Spitfire over Dunkirk, 23 May 1940 (p44). An
experienced pilot, he had spent several years in the pre-war RAF, though this was

his first combat. On 23 May he shot down three enemy aircraft including this Me110.
Painting: Robert Taylor © The Military Gallery

SBD Dauntless dive-bombers based on the USS *Lexington* during the Battle of the Coral Sea (pp201–203). As well as the usual stress of combat, these crews faced the

danger that their 'landing strip' could suddenly be destroyed – as happened here.
Painting: Robert Taylor © The Military Gallery

Harold 'Mick' Martin's Lancaster completes a successful run on the Mohne Dam during the famous 'Dambusters' raid, one of Bomber Command's greatest triumphs

and most well-known actions. The glory, however, proved expensive: eight of the nineteen crews involved were lost. *Painting: Robert Taylor © The Military Gallery*

German Me109s dice with Russian Yaks on the Eastern Front. Luftwaffe pilots considered their Soviet opponents greatly inferior in ability, training and equipment,

though as the war progressed the Russians became a more experienced and dangerous enemy. *Painting: Robert Taylor (detail)* © *The Military Gallery*

Denis Crowley-Milling briefs pilots of 181 Squadron (pp49–50). A career
pilot who ultimately became an Air Marshal, he was the founder of this highly
successful Typhoon squadron.

Hugh 'Cocky' Dundas (p48). Battle of Britain pilots were famous
for a cavalier informality of dress, typified by scarves and a left-
undone top tunic button.

Paddy Barthrop (second from left) with other RAF pilots in a POW camp
in Poland, 1943 (pp70–71). In spite of capture and incarceration, many RAF
prisoners-of-war retained an unmistakeable swagger.

Group Captain Denys Gillam briefing 146 Wing RAF pilots, Antwerp,
1945 (p30). These men had progressed from Hurricanes and Spitfires to
Typhoons which, in the later stages of the European war, gave invaluable
support to Allied armies and proved the scourge of the retreating Germans.

Top scoring Allied fighter pilot Johnnie Johnson with the defiant message 'Bader's Bus Co Still Running' on the side of his Spitfire (p65). He was one of several pilots who had learned his trade through flying with Bader and who went on to a distinguished career of service – in his case 38 'kills' and the eventual rank of Air Vice-Marshal.

Robert Fumerton with a piece of a shot-down Ju88, June 1941 (p173). Latching on to this aircraft, he raked it with bullets until it exploded, providing a first 'kill' for his 496 Squadron Beaufighter.

Though all of this crew survived, it was a German and not an Allied air-sea rescue craft that found them.

The nearer a flyer came to completing his tour the more imperative survival became.

DONALD H SMITH, USAAF

I recognized an increasing dread of future missions as I progressed further into my tour, having seen many of the disastrous consequences of close-formation flying and effective enemy fire.

When the longed-for moment came, and the tour was finished, one man responded with a weary quip:

On our return to our revetment at home base, one crew member refused to get on the truck that would take us to the debriefing centre. He said, looking at the truck-bed: 'I'm never going to get that high off the ground again.'

To last through that many missions was asking a great deal of any man's nerve, but to refuse to go was not an option.

Under penalty of court martial a pilot could not turn back from a mission if his plane would fly. Even complete failure of electrical, navigational, radio, armament equipment was not sufficient excuse to return to base. Engine failure was just about the only justification.

Invariably some felt they could not go on, and were willing to lose not only their rank but their membership of this close-knit body.

BILL ETHERIDGE, USAAF

One crew member decided that he could no longer fly in combat. He reported to headquarters the next day, stated his decision and

offered up his non-com rank. Subsequently he was demoted to Private and was assigned to various non-flying tasks. Not wanting anyone who could not face up to the risks ahead, Mateyka called the remaining crew members together and simply stated that if anyone wanted to transfer he should go immediately . . .

Those who flew the missions were helped to survive by a deliberately-cultivated and highly-necessary sense of indifference both to the fate of other crews and those on whom their bombs fell.

DONALD H SMITH, USAAF

Humour in the service became quite coarse. Complaints or statements were sometimes met with 'Tell it to the Chaplain' or, more often, 'Let me punch your card for you.'

We all carried emergency TS (tough shit) cards. Don't ask me where the expression originated. Lack of sympathy by others toward one's personal problems supposedly contributed to mental toughness.

My feelings about dropping death-dealing bombs on to targets below? Guilt? Sorrow? Anger? Revenge? The answer – none of the above. This was what I had been trained, for over two years, to do. My lack of emotion was surely due in part to the fact that we were so detached, at altitudes of five miles or higher, from the destruction and devastation below. If anti-aircraft fire was heavy at the moment of bomb release, fear might dominate; otherwise, there was a mixed feeling of satisfaction at having gotten the job done, and relief in the assumption that we were more than halfway through the flak-zone, and that engine failure was less likely at the reduced power now necessary.

I think the two dominating feelings during missions were commitment and determination to get the bombs on the target, and survival. It was facetiously said that 'You are working for Uncle Sam until "Bombs Away", then you are working for yourself!'

I do not recall ever meeting anyone during my military experiences whose conscience troubled him about taking action against an enemy – rather, the more effective the action, the better.

However much this outlook may have helped bomber crews to survive a tour, there is no question that the cost of their victory was immense.

BILL CLUTTERHAM, USAAF

There were thousands of pilots that were killed in action. On a single raid over Germany as many as 300 B-17s would not make it home. They went down in flames. Three hundred planes, six hundred pilots, two thousand four hundred air crew members. Three hundred planes meant a total of three thousand men who died on one mission. War is brutal. It is staggering to consider the losses. A class of pilots graduating from flying-training usually consisted of 200 men who were Second Lieutenants. One bombing mission and three classes of pilots gone, KIA.

4

THE WIDER CONFLICT

With the end of Hitler's air assault on Britain, other fields of strife opened up. Germany's ally, Italy, sought to drive the British from North Africa and seize the Suez Canal. The British-held island of Malta, a vital outpost in the Mediterranean, was subjected to siege and bombardment. Over a period of two years Malta became a second Battle of Britain, savagely bombed by Axis forces flying from Sicily and Libya. It was defended by British and Commonwealth fighter pilots, and supplied by convoys that ran the gauntlet of German U-boats. These not only fed the population but replaced losses in pilots and planes. The attacks failed, and its successful resistance against a determined and able foe added more laurels to the RAF's reputation.

In Africa, aircraft had a vital reconnaissance role in the vast and featureless desert. Pilots flew raids, and dogfights were common when the two sides met. The war was dominated, however, by armour and artillery, and flyers largely settled into the function that they would fulfil for the rest of the conflict – supporting ground troops.

They followed their respective armies through the two years of back-and-forth fighting between Tobruk and El Alamein and, when the Allies won in Africa and took the war back to Europe in the summer of 1943, the RAF and US Army Air Force protected the landings at Salerno and Anzio. When Italy came over to the Allies, the Germans dug in across the Italian peninsula and resisted ferociously, tying down Anglo-American troops until Germany itself was overrun and their leaders ordered them to surrender. From Italian airfields the Allied air forces were able to mount raids into southern Germany, bringing devastation to Munich and other cities whose remoteness from England had given them a relative degree of security.

The war's biggest battlefield was the Soviet Union, and this was a war of extremes. The distances were enormous, the climate – in summer or winter – a gruelling test of endurance. The amounts of men and *materiel* deployed by both protagonists dwarfed in size anything seen on other fronts. There was no respect between the two sides, and atrocities, perpetrated by both, were commonplace. The casualties were mind-boggling but it was here on the Eastern Front, at a cost of perhaps 27,000,000 Soviet lives, that Hitler was decisively beaten.

The Luftwaffe began with a huge advantage: the surprise attack on 22 June 1942 enabled them to destroy a large percentage of the Soviet Air Force, much of it on the ground. Over the following weeks and months it pursued the retreating enemy in tandem with the ground forces, and enjoyed virtual air superiority. Russian airmen were less well-trained, less experienced and flying inferior machines – a situation that changed only gradually as imported Western aircraft, and the development of their own expertise, began to take effect. Soviet pilots fought with tremendous courage but, as with their compatriots on the ground, countless lives were thrown away to stall the advancing Germans.

Hitler's defeat began in the air, for it was Goering's rash assurance that the Luftwaffe could supply the entire Seventh Army at Stalingrad that committed him to that action. Once the tide had turned, the Luftwaffe, like the rest of the *Wehrmacht*, conducted a fighting retreat that lasted more than two years and took them all the way back to Berlin.

For German pilots the war in the East was difficult and dangerous. Their living conditions were usually primitive, their aircraft were often rendered unreliable by the climate, and they were the constant target of partisans, who could destroy a plane with small-arms fire as it took off or landed. If they were captured they could well be torn to pieces by an angry mob; bailing out over enemy territory was something that no pilot wanted to think about. Nevertheless, the Eastern front was rewarding in terms of 'kills'. Many German aces reached their three-figure totals in that theatre.

Western Europe became a major battleground again with the Allied invasion of Normandy on 6 June 1944. The RAF and USAAF not only kept enemy aircraft away from the landing, but devastated the retreating German columns as they struggled along the narrow country roads. Equipped with long-range petrol tanks and capable of firing rockets or dropping bombs, a new generation of fighters proved to be a decisive force in the swift advance of Allied armies across the Continent. As the Luftwaffe ran short of fuel, aircraft and pilots, the Anglo-Americans came close to achieving air superiority. Fighters could accompany the bomber formations all the way to Berlin, and the sight of them over the city led Goering to admit that the war was lost. The fighter aircraft, seen in 1940 as a symbol of dogged resistance, had five years later become, for one Nazi at least, a symbol of Allied victory.

* * *

Pilots' memories of the Middle East war tended to be dominated by the types of aircraft they – and their opponents – flew, as much as by the action they saw. As happened throughout the conflict, flyers might struggle with outdated machines until these were replaced by more efficient craft. The interception of a German reconnaissance aircraft earned one member of the RAF the personal gratitude of the Naval C-in-C:

WOODY WOODWARD, RAF

One of my most satisfying combats was my last one. On 12 July 1941, I was one of the two pilots 'scrambled' over Alexandria to catch a Ju88 engaged in reconnaissance. Unlike earlier sorties, this was a controlled interception, with HMS *Formidable* tracking the enemy and vectoring me about the sky.

The '88 was on the same level as myself when I spotted him. As soon as I fired he went over and straight down, levelling out near the desert. I had followed closely. Two more bursts and the Junkers caught fire and crashed. I received a message of thanks from Admiral Sir Andrew Cunningham for that episode.

The four-gun Gloster Gladiator, which I flew until October 1940, was delightful to handle, but even at the outset of the North African campaign we recognized that it was obsolete. We could shoot down CR32s with relative ease, but a well-piloted CR42 could be troublesome. Modern bombers like the BR20 were difficult to intercept. I never had to fly Gladiators against German machines.

Flying Hurricanes was much more business-like; the effect of those eight machine guns on vehicles could be spectacular. Unfortunately, my most intensive operational time on Hurricanes was in Greece, when everything was in the enemy's favour. Even in 1943 I was still on the type; by then Spitfires had assumed the burden of aerial fighting in the Mediterranean.

Another flyer described, with laconic professional slang, a duel with an Italian fighter over Tobruk.

WALLY CONRAD, RAF

On 27 March 1942, while on an interception patrol near Tobruk, I became separated from the squadron while chasing a Hun through the sand haze. While doing a spiral climb to get above the haze, I spotted a Macchi 202 apparently stalking me on the outside of my turn. We began to dice, and it was the only time that I recall when I found myself in a one-to-one situation with both pilots ready to fight it out. After a few minutes of ineffective sparring, it was apparent that pilots and aircraft were fairly matched. Then the Italian decided (he told us later) that he was getting low on fuel and should break it off by doing a 'falling leaf'. It was a stupid mistake, because I first dropped some flap, waiting for him to recover, and hose-piped him from dead astern. He started to smoke and drove away into the haze. The pilot bailed out and was picked up by our army. When interrogated, the cheeky beggar said he'd been shot down by a Spitfire. He insisted that no Hurricane had been built that could beat a Macchi.

Meanwhile, the epic siege of Malta had begun. Pilots who had won their spurs over France and England now found themselves fighting an equally relentless war to defend the island against air raids.

LADDIE LUCAS, RAF

After training in Canada in 1940, I served my apprenticeship with Fighter Command's 66 Squadron in 1941 before being posted, in early 1942, to Malta. I was later given command of 249, often claimed to be the Royal Air Force's top-scoring fighter squadron, at the height of the island battle.

I recall well one incident in the intense fighting. The Squadron, brilliantly controlled from the ground by Group Captain Woodhall, was perfectly positioned to meet an incoming raid of three Italian Cant bombers, closely attended by the Luftwaffe's 70-plus Me109 escort. With height and sun on its side, the Squadron cut clean through the fighter screen to send all three bombers plunging earthwards. It was a model interception.

NIP HEPPELL, RAF

On 10 March 1942, Stan Turner, from Canada, was leading our Squadron and I was leading a section of four Spitfires. We climbed to over 20,000ft to try and intercept some enemy bombers and fighters, but there was a lot of cloud about and I had difficulty keeping contact with Turner. After some time searching for him I suddenly saw eight enemy aircraft about 3 or 4,000ft below and led my flight to attack. I got in a long burst at the leading Messerschmitt and could see I was hitting him, but I was closing very fast and suddenly I must have hit his slipstream because my Spitfire was wrenched upside down and I thought I had been shot at and hit from behind. I pulled into a steep turn, jettisoned the canopy and called my wingman to report any damage, but he replied that all was well, and that he had seen the 109 crash into the Grand Harbour. This was the first Spitfire victory over Malta.

After landing we held a post mortem about my losing contact with Stan Turner. Clearly, this was my fault and we all put it down to 'finger trouble', but two days later another pilot, flying the same Spitfire, flopped out of a formation at 25,000ft and just regained consciousness at low level. Inspection revealed that the oxygen supply was faulty, and we concluded that I was suffering from oxygen starvation when I lost contact with Turner.

MOOSE FUMERTON, RCAF

In retrospect, my most important encounters occurred at Malta in late June and early July, 1942. The fate of the island was of great consequence to the fighting in North Africa. 89 Squadron had set up a detachment of five Beau's called 'C' Flight on 22 June, and in the following few nights I had shot down five enemy aircraft. On the night of 3 July the usual force of enemy aircraft took off from Sicily bound for Malta. Bing and I intercepted the leading aircraft and I opened fire from a range of 75 yards. It was a dark night, but for a few seconds a tremendous explosion turned night into day. I instantly pulled up to avoid the heavy debris, at the same time turning back for the next interception. I was astounded to find that all the raiders, with full bomb-loads, had turned back, diving for home. As far as I was concerned they were quite safe; my windshield was coated with oil from the exploded Ju88. The raids continued, but I had the distinct feeling that the enemy was flying more cautiously.

On the night of 2–3 March 1942, I was sent up (with Sergeant Bing as an observer) to intercept a hostile raider over the Suez Canal and eventually spotted the enemy, but my Beaufighter was standing out against the desert sand in the bright moonlight. An eclipse of the moon had started, however, so I waited for the light to tone down a bit. I then closed in to 100 yards and opened fire, scoring hits. At the same time, the enemy fired back, hitting me in the leg and putting the starboard motor and reflector gun-sight out of action. My aircraft filled with smoke from incendiary bullets.

I opened the side vents. The smoke cleared and I saw the enemy aircraft 200 yards ahead and 100ft above. I pulled up into firing position and began firing, aiming by tracer effect. Meanwhile the enemy was firing back and my port engine cut. As I fell away I saw flames coming from the Heinkel's port engine. When the second engine cut, I pushed the nose down steeply to keep the flying speed up. I turned the landing lights on to land and saw palm trees and canals (a pleasant enough sight on some other occasion!). At that moment my port engine sputtered and began running.

By the racket it made I knew that it was badly damaged but I managed to keep the air speed up to 117mph (just above stall) and the altitude at 200ft (too low for radio contact). It wasn't possible at that speed to turn without stalling. The only aerodrome on course that I could possibly make was Idku, located near Alexandria on a salt flat. It was 100 miles away and we had to hit it right on the nose the first time. Because of the low air-speed, and the lack of hydraulics, I had to fly the Beau right on to the ground without wheels or flaps, cutting the ignition switches eight-feet above the ground. It was a rough landing. I was told later that the engine that started up and brought us in had five bullet holes in the cylinders.

Fighting in North Africa veered between victory and defeat for both sides. A pilot described the role of the RAF during a major Allied reverse:

JOHN WADDY, RAF

I was a pilot of 260 Squadron, Kittyhawks, and with ten victories at this time was a confident and experienced fighter pilot. The Eighth Army were retreating from El Agheila to El Alamein; the enormous tank battle at Knightsbridge had been fought and lost, and we were dive-bombing and strafing Rommel's advancing columns. I was leading my section of four Kittyhawks back to base at 3,000ft when suddenly, without warning, I saw my wingman, about 100 yards away, going down in flames with two Messerschmitt 109s on his tail. I swung in behind the last 109, opened fire and hit him, but after a few rounds all six machine guns jammed and I, the hunter, soon became the quarry.

On my left, a few miles away, was the Mediterranean. Not far inland were three escarpments about 150ft high, running roughly parallel to the shore. I was flying about 20ft above the ground with my right-hand wing tucked in as far as safety permitted to the escarpment, with the leading 109 about 100 yards behind me. His wingman was about the same distance away, on the top of the escarpment. Thus, the wingman could not get at me and the leader had to be very careful of my slipstream. Under the circumstances I thought I was in the safest possible position, but a continuous series of bangs and thumps made me very much aware that I was being hit.

Suddenly the escarpment flattened out and there I was: at low level, no guns, two Messerschmitts on my tail and nothing but flat ground ahead. I was not afraid but bloody angry, and I broke to the left in a steep climb, turning, which seemed to take both 109s by surprise. Having gained a valuable few yards I then dived back to the deck with the 109s following right behind to my airfield, and as I crossed it at about ten feet, they fired their last bursts.

The Commanding Officer was just getting out of his Kittyhawk when he saw me coming and a line of bullets throwing up the dust across the landing strip and coming in his direction, and I can see him now diving face-first into the thick dust.

On landing, I was inspecting my Kitty, which was scarred by more than 120 bullet-holes, when the CO sent for me and gave me a good dressing down for bringing the Messerschmitts back to our airfield, but he never explained where I should have led them!

On 12 May 1942, eight of our long-range Kittyhawks escorted five Beaufighters to try and intercept Ju52s carrying reinforcements

and supplies to Rommel, operating between Crete and Derna. Soon
after reaching our patrol line I saw a gaggle of Ju52s approaching
head-on. I made a complete circuit of the enemy (three-engine
transports on this occasion, carrying troops), but without seeing
any fighter escort. Then followed a furious few minutes in which
I destroyed two Ju52s and two Me100s and was myself hit by return
fire. When I left the fight only three enemy aircraft were still flying
and I counted nine aircraft burning in the sea below.

Malta continued to hold out, in spite of a battering more terrible than the
London Blitz.

ROBERT MIDDLEMISS, RCAF

On 7 July 1942, along with nine other pilots I sat at readiness when
the order came through to scramble eight aircraft leaving Daddo
Langlois and myself on the ground. At that time on the George
Cross Island the saying was 'It was safer in the air than on the
ground' – and we persuaded the controller to let us take off to join
the others . . . the delay, however, cost us time, which meant gaining
height for a good attack position. We spotted the bombers, Ju88s, on
the same level as ourselves, which meant the enemy fighters must
be above us ready to pounce. Daddo said, 'Shall we have a go?'
I said: 'Let's get them!' The account of what followed is in my
combat report.

Combat Report: 7 July 1942 – Malta
. . . Daddo turned in and got one of the 88s, unaware that a
109 had him in his sights. Seeing this, I attacked and saw strikes
along the enemy aircraft. I knew, of course, that his buddy could
not be far away and checked over my shoulder. Suddenly, my
right hand left the stick with the impact of my having been shot
in the right arm and back. I was in a spin, unable to eject because
of the centrifugal force, but managed to roll the Spitfire over

and fall free out of the plane to land in the Mediterranean. Now to inflate the dinghy. The words went through my mind – 'slowly turn the tap of the CO bottle.' After frantically turning the tap this way and that I realized the CO bottle was empty – no help there. With great difficulty, due to my injuries, I managed to pump some air into the dinghy and started to paddle towards the island. To make my problem worse, the squadron were looking for me on the other side of the island and it was only when Paul Brennan and Ray Hesselyn flew out to protect the minesweepers that they spotted me floating in the ocean. I was later picked up by Air Sea Rescue.

My injuries sustained during this combat necessitated my leaving the island and it was back to England for me, where I instructed at OTU for a short time.

ROD SMITH, RCAF

Throughout July, Malta was receiving four or five bombing raids a day. On 24 July, I shot down a Ju88 almost over our aerodrome, expending all my cannon shells and putting it on fire. It left a long arc of black smoke that lasted a long time. Between that day and the end of October I shot down two more Ju88s, a tri-motored Italian SM79 and two Me109Fs. Daylight bombing began again in October, and I became a flight commander in the squadron. On 15 October I was shot down, baled out, fell into the sea and luckily was rescued. In December 1942, I returned to England to spend most of 1943 instructing at a Hurricane OTU and taking leave in Canada.

During the daylight bombing of Malta in October 1942 my Squadron intercepted nine Ju88s escorted by 80 Me109Fs, attacking from one side. I flew across and behind the 88s to fire at the one on the far side. The gunners in the 88s fired tracer bullets at me, which looked like coils of thrown rope. The 109s were swarming above and behind me, and after I fired at my 88 and set its port engine on fire, I saw tracer from 109s going right over my head towards the 88. I dived down for several seconds then came back up again to fire at the starboard engine of the 88, which caught fire also. The 88 plunged gracefully down and exploded spectacularly before falling into the sea. It was the first Hun bomber to come down in the October blitz.

A major contribution to the Allied effort in the desert was made by South African squadrons. A member of one recalled the seemingly endless, but highly necessary, training he underwent as wingman to the commanding officer.

NATHANIEL FLEKSER, RAF

Hour after hour, day after day, Tiny [Nel] and I practised. His wing became the focus of my universe – even my dreams. I learned to tuck my wing behind his and keep station. I had a problem staying with him as he tightened his turn. I began to black out and had to break off. I learned how to breathe in short, sharp, rapid gasps, feeding my oxygen-starved brain.

The tight turn was our most important defensive manoeuvre. The German Messerschmitts were faster than our Hurricanes. They out-climbed and out-dived us, but we could outrun them. A German pilot who tried to match our rate of turn as we poured on the 'G' forces would develop a high-speed stall and spin out.

Much of his time in the air was spent in reconnaissance and in support of ground troops:

We never flew together in squadron-strength – our missions were performed in pairs. The leader's attention was focused on gathering information. The wingman kept a sharp lookout for enemy aircraft.

. . . I learned to identify and count tanks, guns and vehicles, direct artillery shoots and perform aerial photography. But the art of survival was never broached. One simply did not talk of such things in upper-crust British Army circles.

Encounters with enemy fighters were not necessarily an everyday occurrence:

> This was not like the movies, where every second is crammed full of air battles, danger and death. The sky is a great big lonely place. Most of the time the Messerschmitts didn't find us – they couldn't be everywhere, all the time . . .

. . . but ground fire could be a continuing problem.

> Another time . . . an anti-aircraft shell exploded near my Hurricane and sent a piece of shrapnel through my steel seat, into my buttock. I still have the scar. Somehow a shot in that quarter is associated with the cowardly act of running away – an indication of a yellow streak. A battle wound elsewhere is regarded as an act of bravery. I would much rather have taken that wound in a fleshy part of the arm.

Flekser survived, only to be shot down and captured a short time later. He was surprised to hear that the man responsible wanted to meet him, and that this pilot turned out to be the Luftwaffe's highest-scoring flyer in the Middle Eastern theatre. His recent adversary explained to him a crucial point about the German approach to combat flying – the reason why Luftwaffe aces had much higher tallies of 'kills' than their Allied counterparts:

> 'I am Hans Marseilles; you are number 56.' He saw the look of disbelief on my face and said: 'You British pilots fly a tour of 50 sorties, and then retire from combat. We Germans continue to fly. The more we fly, the more experienced and effective we

become. That is why Germany is winning the war. I have flown over 200 sorties.'

Marseilles, who earned the title 'The Star of Africa', reached a score of 158 before being killed in a flying accident.

Eventually, following the arrival of American troops and the appointment of Montgomery, the tide of war turned in the Allies' favour, though the cost – as one Wing Commander reflected – was very high.

BERT HOULE, RAF

Later I was posted to 213 Squadron where we flew Hurricane IIcs with the two outboard cannons removed. This did not give much of a fire pattern and we were almost helpless against the much faster, higher-flying Me109s. My first success came on 1 September 1942, when I was leading ten Hurries against a Ju88 bomber raid on our El Alamein line. After a short burst my cannon seized, and as my fighter had been hit by return fire I returned to base where my number three confirmed the kill. During this engagement we destroyed three enemy aircraft but we lost five Hurries – two pilots were killed and three managed to walk back. I was Acting Flight Commander at the time while the other Flight Commander was 'Jock' Cameron, later Sir Neil Cameron, GCB, CBE, DSO, DFC, ADC, Chief of the Air Staff

When Wing Commander Darwen took over the Spitfire wing in November 1942, he took me with him as Flight Commander in 145 Squadron, and I managed to destroy another 109 before going off for a rest in 1943. A review of those officers with me at that time will indicate how dangerous war can be. Wing Commander Darwin was later killed in Italy, and his replacement, Wing Commander Ian Gleed, was killed before the fall of Tunis; his replacement, Wing Commander Oliver, was shot down over Sicily and became a POW. My CO, Roy Marples, was killed in the UK and his replacement, Lance Wade, was killed in Italy. Our other Flight Commander, John Taylor, was killed in Sicily.

My most memorable action was on 26 October 1942, when at dusk, I got into about two squadrons of Ju87s flying west into an illuminated sky while I was in relative darkness. On the first three I got so close that the bullets straddled the target. Slight right rudder put the left cannon on target. On the fourth Stuka I inadvertently pushed forward on the stick: the result was spectacular. Each cannon fired into a wing-root fuel cell. They both blew up. I watched mesmerized while the aircraft went into a slow spiral from about 700ft and crashed on a sandy spit. I damaged another enemy aircraft, then throttled back and headed for home. Germany has admitted the loss of two pilots that night and that the two gunners bailed out. No one had admitted to the flamer as yet. I was awarded the DFC for this action.

The Axis siege of Malta had failed. It was now Sicily and Italy that faced attack.

HAP KENNEDY, RCAF

As the Malta blitz was over late in 1942, our flying was largely offensive over the sea and Sicily, where we encountered Me109s and Junkers 88s and even rarely an old Junkers 52. With 249 Squadron, I quickly learned that with a proper quarter-attack the gyro gun-sight was deadly accurate. I found that I could attack a Junkers 88 and set one engine on fire very quickly, although I must acknowledge that their return fire was very accurate. In Malta I was lucky enough to shoot down seven enemy aircraft and share two others, and was awarded the DFC.

The war in North Africa was lost by the Axis powers on the ground and not in the air, where the Luftwaffe had proved highly effective. Despite its success, however, German flyers had to withdraw to Italy as the conflict moved on to Europe.

ERNST-WILHELM REINERT, LUFTWAFFE

In December 1942, the 2nd Gruppe of JG77, in which I flew in
the 4th Squadron, was removed from Russia and transferred to
Tripolitania, North Africa. We later withdrew to Tunisia. After Russia
the contrast was like that between night and day. I had my most
successful period in Africa and as a consequence I was promoted
to Leutnant in April 1943. In four months I achieved 51 aerial
victories, of which 47 were fighter aircraft. These made me the
most successful fighter pilot in North Africa during that period.

Though this record did not prevent him from making a precipitate exit
from Africa . . .

In May 1943 we left the Cap-bon Peninsula of Tunisia and
transferred, first of all, to Trapani, Sicily, and later to southern
Italy, from where we were pushed ever more quickly northwards.
On 13 August 1943 I was forced to make an emergency landing in
the sea and was barely able to save myself from drowning . . .

These swift departures involved not only evacuating aircraft but
accommodating individual passengers in highly uncomfortable
circumstances.

At the end of the African Campaign, at the beginning of May,
my Wing was forced to move hastily to Sicily to continue the
fight against the Allies. Then came a special mission. In order to
get everybody out, we had to make extra room in our Me109s.
Therefore, we removed the armour plating in the cockpit roof. One
man then knelt behind the pilot. In the fuselage, a third man hung
on to the second, which made it necessary to remove the radio.

On the afternoon of 8 May 1943, I had to give up my own badly
damaged aircraft, because, shortly after I landed, another aircraft
crashed into it and both were destroyed. I therefore climbed into

the Me109G-6 'Yellow 7', belonging to Leutnant Zeno Bäumel.

Bäumel knelt behind me and our mechanic, Feldwebel Walter, lay behind him. We took off and flew in the general direction of Sicily, hampered by compass trouble.

Over the Mediterranean, I spotted a formation of Grumman Martlets and cautiously approached them from behind. After several minutes in formation, one of the British naval aircraft began to fall behind, so I seized the opportunity to place myself in his blind spot and fired a few bursts. The fighter promptly fell away in flames and I departed hastily northwards at very low level. Bäumel was wildly enthusiastic, but Walter, who couldn't see a thing, was terrified. When we arrived at Trapani, I couldn't resist demonstrating my victory with a low-level pass, my comrades on the ground believing me to have gone mad. After landing safely with a flat tyre, Bäumel was able to confirm my 51st and last victory of the North African Campaign, taking my total to 154.

Allied flyers followed the fighting to mainland Italy. This combat report was submitted after a dogfight.

STOCKY EDWARDS, RCAF

We were patrolling just off Anzio and down the coast at 14,000ft waiting to escort our B-26s over their target. Bandits were reported in the area at 15,000. While flying north we spotted more than 20 Me109s, and long-nosed FW190s come down through the cloud at approximately two o'clock to the section about 500 above. They appeared to be manoeuvring into the sun to bounce the Kitties below. We climbed into the enemy aircraft, closing around to astern. One Me109 was attempting to fire at one of us from 150 yards astern when I fired from 300 astern. I could not observe any hits, but he broke away immediately and went down. I turned on to another, which half-rolled and I fired from about 300 yards. Pieces appeared to fall off and it dived vertically but my cannons stuck in the on position (probably frozen) and did not observe results after it reached 6,000, map reference F7729. I pulled up again and peeled off on another long-nosed FW-190 and chased it to deck level over the coast. Closed to about 300 yards just before crossing our lines. The enemy aircraft saw my Spit behind and took evasive action by weaving violently. I fired two bursts of machine gun from astern. The aircraft poured black smoke, caught fire, the pilot tried to side-slip the flames away but hit the deck and crashed at map reference F8440. I claim one FW-190 (long-nosed) destroyed and one FW-190 (l-n) damaged.

Damage was later confirmed by the Army – in fact, six enemy aircraft were shot down and only four claims made.

. . . and actions of this sort were a continuing aspect of the Italian campaign.

HAP KENNEDY, RCAF

On October 13 1943, I was leading a flight over the Volturno River when two Me109s attacked from the rear, so we turned into them and they overshot. We pursued them down to 500ft and I got a few good strikes on one whose pilot baled out and bounced along the ground just as his chute was opening.

We returned to the Volturno at 8,000ft when a further 12 109s dived down on us and, again, we turned into them. In the ensuing scrap Jock (Red Two) lost me and I was alone. The 109s, in three sections of four, and I turned steeply, climbing all the time, and my superior climb was my best weapon. Suddenly they dived to the north and I followed. They levelled off at about 2,000ft and throttled back. Just as I came within range they obligingly moved into a tight formation to put on a show for their ground crews and as we crossed their grass airfield I let 'arse-end Charlie' have a blast. My starboard cannon jammed, the Spitfire yawed and

I missed him, but I quickly compensated, fired again, hit him
and pulled hard to starboard. Looking over my shoulder, I saw
a parachute floating down.

Italy broke the 'Pact of Steel' and joined the Allied side, though fighting
continued there until the European war ended.

The Mediterranean war also included the Balkans. In Yugoslavia,
German ground troops fought a particularly vicious breed of partisan.
Understandably, flyers hoped never to be shot down over this region.
One had a very fortunate escape:

JOHANNES STEINHOFF, LUFTWAFFE

When I was stationed in Italy, commanding JG77, I had one
Gruppe based in Romania. To visit them, we had to cross the
'Bomber Avenue', the daily flight path the bombers were taking
towards Germany.

En route one day, I had to cross Yugoslavia, which was full of
bandits who treated the prisoners in a horrible way. Arriving over
Agram/Zagreb with four Messerschmitts, I saw Lightnings in the
vicinity. Forgetting that my aircraft was loaded with Cognac for my
Third Gruppe, I attacked. The first one went down trailing thick
smoke and I immediately attacked the next one. Then came an
urgent warning from my wingman: 'Macky, watch it!' The offending
aircraft hit me on a collision course. Suddenly, at 20,000ft, I was
engulfed in smoke and I couldn't see anything.

Quickly losing altitude and needing to get as far eastward as
possible, I switched off the engine to try to get the heat-level down.
I was flying over bandit country. Getting lower, I could make out a
green field in front of me which I elected to land in. But everything
happened too fast and I landed with a tremendous crash. Quickly
releasing the harnesses, I jumped to the ground to find myself
surrounded by German firemen! I had landed on the only German
airfield in northern Yugoslavia. Boy, was I lucky!

For Hitler, however, Italy and the Balkans were mere sideshows. The most important campaign had been launched in June 1941, when his troops invaded Russia. This was his chance to come to grips with his real enemy – Communism – and to gain for Germany the living space that had been his primary objective in going to war. The Soviets, who were his allies, were caught entirely by surprise and German forces, particularly in the air, were extremely successful.

DIETER HRABAK, LUFTWAFFE

We received the new, more streamlined and powerful 109F in preparation for the invasion of Russia. It was a highly capable aircraft which was easily able to deal with the challenge from the Soviet aircraft, many of which were obsolete [though], as the war progressed, this situation changed.

GUNTHER RALL, LUFTWAFFE

In May 1941, I flew in support of the attack on Crete and then returned to Romania. At the outbreak of the Russian campaign we were re-equipped with the Me109 and went on the offensive and, operating from Romania on the Black Sea, my squadron concentrated on Russian bombers, shooting down nearly 50 in one week. Later, I participated in the German attack through the Ukraine and the Crimean peninsula towards Taganrog.

Returning to 8./JG 52, I took part in the attack on Rostov and the fighting in the Caucasus, reaching my 100th victory in October 1942, for which I received the Oak Leaves to the Knight's Cross. I then took part in the attack on Stalingrad before my unit withdrew to Nikolayev for refurbishment. Later, during the fighting in the so-called Kuban Bridgehead, I had my first contact in the East with Western-built Spitfires . . .

FRIEDRICH OBLESER, LUFTWAFFE

In my wing, the standard aircraft we flew on the Eastern Front was the Me109F and the Me109G to G-6, receiving each new model without any special conversion training. The performance of the Me109 was sufficient for aerial combat with the Russian fighters until about mid-1944, after which they met us on even terms. Our standard weaponry was one 20mm cannon and two 13mm machine guns, sometimes with two 20mm cannon in pods under the wings. These were very effective against larger targets but impaired manoeuvrability and rate of climb. From late 1943 we had a new 30mm engine-mounted cannon with a 60-round drum which, although very powerful, was not ideal for fighter versus fighter combat, since the trajectory of the rounds was not straight enough.

DIETHELM VON EICHEL-SCHREIBER, LUFTWAFFE

We attacked Russia on the first day and destroyed Russian planes in great numbers on the ground. They were still standing lined up and unprotected. One day we protected German bombers (three squadrons) and when we came back they had doubled in numbers. What had happened was that a group of Russian twin-engine bombers had come down where our bombers flew in order to attack our airfield at Yasi. Alex said 'Get them!' and we all three squadrons attacked the Russians. Alex got six or more and I got six or more and our group members shot a great number. The Russian group was destroyed. A photographer from the *Volkisher Beobachter* who had photographed me put it all in the paper. Alex said, 'Let's give some of the credit to the young fighter-pilots who had also shot at the bombers.' So we did. We gave half of the shot-down bombers to other members of the group.

ERNST-WILHELM REINERT, LUFTWAFFE

In June 1941, from many different airfields in Romania (a German ally), we flew operations in support of the Russian campaign, generally as escorts for our bombers and Stukas. We also attacked Russian troop concentrations and flew free-hunt missions. I finally shot down my first aircraft on 8 August 1941, and by the end of the year I had shot down 24.

ERICH RUDORFER, LUFTWAFFE

In Usin, Russia, I was ordered to accompany a formation of 30 Stukas with my eight aircraft. As the Stukas began their dive, I suddenly saw about 20 Yaks start to attack and immediately took four aircraft down in front of the Stukas to engage them. At the end of the combat all of the Stukas returned home, but we had virtually wiped out the Russian unit. I myself had shot down six Yak 9s and seven Yak 7s in a period of just 17 minutes. I don't know if any other fighter pilot ever achieved that!

HEINZ LANGE, LUFTWAFFE

In the first week of this war I achieved seven victories, after which I was given command of 1./ JG-54 on 1 October 1941. Thirteen months later I was transferred to command 3./ JG-51, having by this time achieved 20 victories. The following January I was awarded the 500 mission attachment to my Front Clasp in Gold for Fighter Pilots and, a month later, was promoted to Hauptmann. By 22 August 1943, now a holder of the German Cross in Gold, my score of victories had reached 40 and my scoring rate was starting to increase, reaching 50 on 26 October.

Although they might have dominated the skies, Luftwaffe crews dreaded what might await them on the ground. Partisans attacked airfields, and any flyer who came down in Soviet-held territory could expect no mercy if captured by civilians.

ALFRED GRISLAWSKI, LUFTWAFFE

In Russia, the sort of operation that worried us the most was the deep penetration attack on an enemy airfield which could be up to 100 miles behind the enemy lines. The Russian airfields were always

very well protected, with strong ground defences, so we always
required a certain amount of luck to get away. We all worried about
being shot down behind Russian lines.

One German bomber crew had a lucky escape, having suffered an engine
malfunction while flying over partisan territory.

ERICH SCHUDAK, LUFTWAFFE

We took off at dusk on the 4 April in our usual cheerful mood. After
flying for about an hour, the right engine started spitting and we
started to go down. We immediately changed course for home. I sent
off a signal to let them know we were coming back on one engine.
It was acknowledged and we then concentrated on lightening the
aircraft. All my ammunition and an MG went overboard, plus a lot
of other stuff. But we were losing speed; home was not getting any
closer. Luckily we spotted a clearing and, just before we touched
down, I pressed the key and signalled: Belly, Belly and then we
were down . . .

My radio equipment was still intact so I sent a message to give
details of our landing and the estimated location. I wanted to ask
whether we should destroy the plane, but they decided that we
should disappear as secretly and quickly as possible, because we
were in the partisan area. We set off across the frozen swamp
carrying our compass and rucksacks with emergency supplies,
after destroying all evidence of radio messages.

We eventually came upon a path, which led to a village; we did
not stay on it though. It was a miserable march, especially with the
baggage, as we were also carrying two MGs.

I suddenly noticed a farmhouse in the distance. We approached
it and got a very friendly reception. We had some refreshment and
were then driven to the nearest police station. They were most
amazed that the partisans had not attacked us. The navigator and
myself, plus a dozen policemen, went in search of the plane. We

found it [and] loaded everything from the plane into their vehicle to be deposited with them. Estimated worth: RM 100,000.

On the Soviet side, pilots faced a colossal task in attempting to stem the aggressive German onslaught. They suffered from a serious lack of planes and flyers, while outdated aircraft and lack of adequate training often made them easy targets for the Luftwaffe. Oberst Erich Hartmann, who with 352 kills was the war's highest-scoring fighter pilot, gave his views on his Soviet opponents in an interview 20 years after hostilities had ended.

> He attributed his high score to the fact that a fighter ace had to have exceptional skill to survive in the East because there was no specific tour of missions. You were there until you either won or lost completely . . . He also said they had many, many targets and that the average Russian pilot had no intelligence, no initiative, insufficient training and that they used bad tactics. In his estimation they did not have any fighter aircraft that were as good as his Bf109, not even the latest Yaks in 1945.

A colleague made a similar observation.

GERHARD THYBEN, LUFTWAFFE
> It became clear to me that the Russian pilots had much slower reactions than our opponents in the west, who were not taken by surprise so easily.

Erich Hartmann himself put his success down to experience and patience.

ERICH HARTMANN, LUFTWAFFE
> My only tactic was to wait until I had the chance to attack the enemy and then close in at high speed. I opened fire only when the whole windshield was black with the enemy. Wait! – until the enemy covers your wind-shield. Then not a single shot goes wild. The further you

get away from the enemy the less impact and penetration your projectiles have. With the tactic I have described, the enemy aircraft absorbs the full force of your armament at minimum range and it doesn't matter what your angle is to him or whether you are in a turn or any other manoeuvre. When all your guns hit him like this, he goes down! And you have saved your ammunition.

When you begin flying combat and you are a hundred metres from the enemy machine, you get jittery because you are too close to him. By experience you come to know that when you are a hundred metres from the other machine you are still too far away. The inexperienced pilot breaks away for fear of mid-air collision. The experienced pilot brings his machine in much closer . . . and when he fires, the other machine goes down.

In an attempt to bolster the Russian effort, Britain sent both fighters and training staff to northern Russia in 1941. One of them wrote home in highly complimentary terms about his pupils:

WJ FREEMAN, RAF

I have been very busy with the other NCOs instructing Russian mechanics in the care and maintenance of Hurricane aircraft including stopping and starting engines, etc. It has been generally noted by us all [what a] high standard of technical knowledge and efficiency the pilots and mechanics possess. Pilots in the Soviet Air Force undergo two years' training in an engineering school apart from actual flying training.

Twenty Russian pilots arrived for instruction and all [have] done very well . . . plenty of flying was had by the Russian pilots who are learning fast, and 12 new pilots were passed out today after their first experience in a Hurricane.

Their proficiency was put to the test almost immediately when German fighters and bombers raided their airfield. Their teacher was impressed.

Monday was a bright day with brilliant sunshine and Jerry paid us a flying visit with 14 Junkers 88s and 109s. Bombs fell all around doing little damage. Luckily 14 of our machines were already in the air and were quickly joined by others, all gave chase and we have now learned . . . that 12 of the 14 German machines were brought down or badly damaged by our aircraft and AA fire. So ends another expensive raid by Charlie Hitler's air force.

Accounts of the war by Soviet pilots are somewhat scarce, but one aspect of the Eastern Front air war that has been recorded is the use of women as both fighter and bomber aircrew. Unique in aerial combat until the present time, this experiment was successful. There was no lack of volunteers although the danger was considerable. The officer in charge of recruits, a pre-war flyer, left them in no doubt of this.

MARINA RASKOVA, SOVIET AIR FORCE

The girls I choose must understand beyond any doubt whatsoever that they will be fighting against men, and they must themselves fight like men. If you're chosen you may not be killed – you may be burned so your own mother would not recognize you. You may be blinded. You may lose a hand, a leg. You may be captured by the Germans. Do you really want to go through with this?

. . . and they required a softer approach in training, as the second-in-command of their unit recalled.

YEVDOKIA BERSHANSKAYA, SOVIET AIR FORCE.

The girls seemed little more than children in many ways. Training was a very difficult time for all of us. Although most of them were good basic material, with a certain standard in their various skills, they had an awful lot to learn. Marina and I both realized that they needed a certain motherly kindness just as much as they needed to be pushed along with their training.

The need for height or for sheer brute strength could also lead to difficulties, as a bomber pilot remembered.

KATERINA FEDOTOVA, SOVIET AIR FORCE

... fully loaded with bombs, the Pe-2 needed someone with a lot of strength to pull back on the stick at the appropriate moment to get the nose off the ground. Most of us had to get our navigators to stand beside us on take-off to help yank the stick back on a given command. It was a delicate business, though, because if the stick was pulled back too far the aeroplane would lose flying speed, it would stall, and you'd make a big fire on the runway.

Most of us were small girls – quite a bit shorter than the men. We needed cushions to pad our seats so that we could see out of the windscreen. And some of the girls with particularly short legs had to have special blocks put on the rudder pedals so that they could reach them with their feet.

The Pe-2 was not an easy aircraft to take off. Some twin-engined aircraft have the propellers contra-rotating ... which cancels out the tendency of the aircraft to turn in the direction of the propellers; but the Pe-2's props both turned to the left. With both powerful engines on full power for take-off, the bomber had an alarming tendency to swing left. If not controlled quickly and firmly the aircraft would swing off the runway ...

When they encountered the enemy, however, they showed no reluctance to fight. One pilot, flying a Yak over the city of Saratov, saw a German bomber formation below and attacked:

GALIA BOORDINA, SOVIET AIR FORCE

There wasn't really much to think about. I could see them passing below me to the right and left, these vague shapes. I reckoned I must be right in the middle of them. I flicked the guard off the

gun button and pushed the nose straight down. I started firing
right away and, keeping the power full on, I just charged straight
through the middle of the formation. It was terrifying. I passed
very close to one of them as I dived through, then I pulled the stick
back and zoomed up above them again, and did the same thing
again. I don't think I hit any of them with my cannon and machine-
gun fire, but I suspect they thought there was more than one fighter
attacking them. The formation broke up and jettisoned their bombs
in the field. I still had ammunition left, but I couldn't find them
again. A minute or two after my second attack, there was a series
of terrific flashes and explosions as the jettisoned bombs hit
the ground.

While many of the women were flying defensive missions, they also
carried out attacks on enemy targets. This account is of a bombing raid by
Pe-2s in the summer of 1942, and begins by describing the workings of this
classic Soviet aircraft.

YEVDOKIA BERSHANSKAYA, SOVIET AIR FORCE

The Pe-2 carried a crew of three – pilot, navigator and radio
operator/gunner. It had two fixed machine guns firing forward;
one swivelling machine gun in an acrylic plastic bubble behind
the navigator; and two guns operated by the radio operator in
the middle of the fuselage – one in the floor for defence of the
underside of the aircraft, and one that fired through a hatch above
her head. The pilot sat in an armoured seat in the cockpit with the
navigator behind her, also in an armoured seat. The radio operator
sat about six-feet away in the middle of the fuselage, crouched
over her equipment and surrounded by boxes of spare ammunition
belts for her guns.

I felt a fantastic sense of achievement. I could clearly see
the buildings and I knew that if I hit the target then Luba, behind
me, would be able to aim at the fires that I started. The Germans

hadn't heard me coming because of the gliding approach, but now the searchlight came on and the flak started coming up. I realized, as I got more experienced, that this was indeed light opposition, but on that first night it seemed pretty terrifying to me. I didn't want to spoil my aim so I just flew straight on through the explosions until I was right over the target. The aeroplane bucked in the blast from some of the explosions, but we kept on flying. Then I yanked the release wire and dived away from the searchlights and steered for home. I saw flames coming from one of the buildings and thought that Luba would have a beacon to aim for now.

For fighter pilots, dogfighting was as common an experience as it was on the other fronts.

HANNES TRAUTLOFT, LUFTWAFFE

In fighter versus fighter combat, my preference was always for the Me109, due to its high manoeuvrability and particular suitability for tightly turning dogfights. However, it could not absorb a lot of punishment. If the Me109 was a racehorse, then by comparison, the FW-190 was a brave, faithful farm horse. I nevertheless gained great pleasure from flying the FW-190 in Russia because its strong firepower and resistance to being shot-up made it eminently suitable for attacking enemy ground positions and low-flying armour-plated Russian aircraft, such as the Il-2 'Stormovik'. My wing used both aircraft types for fighter bomber operations.

In February 1943, in the midst of winter, my wing received an urgent call for help from troops at the front, who were under air attack. The weather was atrocious, so I took off with my wingman, Feldwebel Forbrig, to check things out. In limited visibility, we flew our FW-190s eastwards at just 100m altitude, navigating by compass.

Reaching the front in just a few minutes, we flew around

low-hanging clouds, occasionally catching glimpses of activity
below. Suddenly, between the snow showers, I caught sight of
two MiGs, which quickly disappeared into cloud. Then Forbrig's
voice alerted me to four enemy Stormoviks flying very low. Diving
to just 100m range, I opened fire and an enemy machine began to
burn, climbing steeply, then spiralling into the ground, near to an
artillery position. A second quickly fell to Forbrig's guns and we
then gave chase to the other two, flying deep into Russian territory,
before being bounced by MiG fighters. After a lengthy dogfight,
Forbrig, hit, announced his departure and I was alone. Then, hit
myself, and with a strong smell of burning, I decided to break off
combat and head for home, only to find, to my horror, that my
compass and blind flying instruments had been destroyed.

In thickening fog, I flew a straight course until hostile fire
from the ground diminished. On close inspection, I discovered that
I was in the Russian hinterland, so I hastily flew the opposite course,
with oil seeping into the cockpit. Eventually crossing our own lines,
unaware of my position, I belly-landed in the first suitable field.
Surveying my wrecked aircraft, a passing infantryman told me I
had been lucky. He was right.

Yet for the Luftwaffe, the war in Russia involved fighting the enemy less
in the skies than on the ground. This pilot gained wide experience of
both, but the emphasis in his narrative on ground attack is typical of the
Eastern Front.

HERMANN BUCHNER, LUFTWAFFE

In March 1942, I was transferred to the Crimean peninsula. From
here I flew my first mission, as a wingman, in the Me109E. Our role
was to support our own ground troops and to attack enemy troop
concentrations, avoiding aerial combat. In the period from May
to December I flew 215 missions, including a forced landing near
Stalingrad on 12 September 1942.

On 29 October 1943, I was wounded in aerial combat and did not return to my squadron for six weeks. In January 1944, my Gruppe was transferred to the Crimea and, up until May, I flew another 180 missions, and was shot down twice, each time making an emergency landing, and destroyed 26 enemy aircraft and 16 tanks. My unit was the last to leave the Crimea, moving on 9 May to Romania to protect the oilfields in the fighter role. Our opponents were American aircraft operating from Italy.

In this area I flew 35 combat missions, destroyed five tanks and shot down eight aircraft. I was also given the leadership of 4./SG-2 Immelmann. On 20 July 1944, I was awarded the Knight's Cross after 500 ground attack missions and 46 aerial victories.

GUNTHER RALL, LUFTWAFFE

Late on a summer afternoon in 1943, during the battle for Kursk, I flew a fighter sweep that took me deep into Russian territory. Flying with my wingman towards a distant tall white cumulus cloud, which was silhouetted by the sun, I spotted two fighter aircraft. Speeding up to close in on them, I could make out large radial engines but, silhouetted from behind, I could not identify the aircraft.

I knew that only a few days before, a unit equipped with the FW-190 had been transferred to our area, but I had never seen one in the air, so I was not sure whether those fighters growing in my gun-sights were Laggs or our own. Closing at high speed, I pulled up and suddenly saw that they were dark green in colour and bore the red markings of the enemy.

I knew that if I used my superior speed to pass him, he would chase me, so I pushed the stick forward and jumped him, firing right into his cockpit. I then pulled the stick hard back, going into a high-speed stall, when a big bang shook my aircraft. The collision between us had cut off his right wing, and his propeller had cut into my lower fuselage.

With only one wing, the Lagg tumbled downwards, spinning

without recovering, but my attention had now turned to the terrible shaking of my engine, which I was anxious not to lose. Lowering the nose to head for our own lines, I adjusted the throttle to try to rescue the vibration, but without success. I landed in a field just behind our lines and, surveying my aircraft, which looked terrible with a long, deep cut underneath, I pulled deeply on a cigarette, happy to be alive.

Whatever their personal success, Luftwaffe pilots could not ignore the colossal defeat their compatriots were suffering on the ground.

DIETER HRABAK, LUFTWAFFE

My own aerial battles never made the impression on me that I received from one stupendous event – Stalingrad. The circumstances after Stalingrad were so terrible as to be indescribable. The plight of my dying, starving countrymen in the snow, and my complete inability to do anything to help is a memory I will carry to my grave. Flying over these scenes of desperate tragedy was a soul-searing experience that is burned into my memory.

The highest-scoring pilot on the Eastern Front – and in the entire war – arrived in Russia in August 1942. He encountered the enemy on his third patrol.

ERICH HARTMANN, LUFTWAFFE

I could not see any enemy aircraft. When we levelled off at high speed, however, I saw two dark-green aircraft in front and a little higher than us at about 3,000m distance. My first thought was, 'Now I must have my first kill.' I put on full power, overtaking my leader to get in front of him for firing position.

I closed very fast and opened fire within about 1,000m range. I watched all my ammunition whizz over and to the left of the target without scoring a hit. The target grew so big so fast that I quickly pulled back on the stick and zoomed upward. Immediately I was surrounded on all sides by dark-green aircraft which quickly turned behind me. I had lost my leader. I climbed through a cloud layer and was all alone.

Then came Rossmann's voice on the RT: 'Don't sweat it. I watched you. Now I've lost you. Come down through the cloud layer so I can pick you up again.'

I dropped down through the cloud layer and saw an aircraft head on to me at about 5,000ft. I was scared stiff and went split-essing downward, heading west and yelling for my leader, telling him that an unknown aircraft was on my tail. Rossmann's voice came back: 'Turn right so I can close.' I turned right, but the machine following me cut across my turn. Now I really panicked. Full power down to low level and head west. I couldn't understand Rossmann's words any more. I kept pulling my head in behind the cockpit armour plate like an ostrich, waiting and dreading the crash of enemy projectiles into my aircraft.

The aircraft stayed behind me, and after a short time I once more heard Rossmann's voice telling me the aircraft on my tail had gone. I climbed again to refix my position, spotted Mount Elbrus to my left and reoriented myself. Then I saw the red fuel warning light glowing in front of me. Five minutes' more flight, then the engine went bang, bang, bang, and quit – I was out of gas.

There were huge sunflower fields below and a road with military trucks. The ground was coming up fast. I bellied-in amid a monstrous dust cloud. I opened the canopy and took out my personal equipment. Army soldiers took me back to the base . . .

That evening there was a big, noisy and uncomfortable debriefing by Major von Bonin, the Gruppen Kommandeur, and then by Rossmann about Rotte tactics. I had committed all the cardinal sins of a tyro fighter pilot, and these were impressed on me with emphatic precision:

1. I separated from my leader.

2. I flew into his firing position instead of protecting him while he did the firing.

3. I climbed through the cloud layer.

4. After descending through the clouds, I escaped from my leader – it was Rossmann who was in the aircraft on my tail.

5. I didn't follow his orders.

6. I lost orientation.

7. I destroyed my own aircraft with nothing to show for it.

After this unpromising start, Hartmann rapidly improved. He remained in Russia for two years, until his unit was overtaken by events. His score, and his prestige, however, continued to expand.

We were forced to hastily depart from [the Crimea] on 8 May 1944, myself flying out with two mechanics in the fuselage of my Me109. By July 1944, my score had reached 266, for which I was awarded the Swords and, on 23 August, I passed the 300 mark. I was the first pilot to do so, for which I was awarded the Diamonds the following day, and ordered by Galland to transfer for training on the Me262. After persistent requests, however, I was able to return to JG-52, this time to command the 4th Squadron.

He fought not only Russians, but Americans in the east.

In late June 1944, I was leading a 'Schwarm' high over the Ploesti Oilfields, as top cover for another 'Schwarm' which was assigned to tackle the approaching American bombers. Diving on a group of four Mustangs, which were attacking our own fighters, I managed to quickly dispose of the rearmost pair at close range, since they had not seen my approach. Before I could turn my attention to a third, however, I received a loud warning over the air from my wingman; 'Behind you! Break! Break!'

I immediately pushed the stick forward, diving down hard, my eyes bulging in their sockets, and went into heavy spirals at full power. Looking in my mirror and quickly from side to side, I could see eight Mustangs behind me. My negative 'G' manoeuvre had given me a slight lead on them, but they had split into two groups and started to close. I began hauling my aircraft, 'Karaya One', into really hard left- and right-hand turns, each time being cut off by gunfire, fortunately not too accurate. I continued to pull blood-draining turns, occasionally firing weapons to try to confuse them. Sweat poured down my face and perspiration ran down my body as I worked to save my life, streaking across the Romanian sky. I had gained a little ground, but the Americans were determined to get me. My only hope was the flak guns at my home base, but this too, was dashed when my low fuel warning light illuminated. I had just one chance. Releasing my safety belt and tripping the emergency canopy release, I pulled hard back on the stick, releasing it when the aircraft was upside-down, and fell to earth. A few moments later, as I swung from my parachute, a Mustang flashed past me, its pilot waving, and the Americans disappeared into the distance.

And it was in the East that his war ended.

In March 1945, I became Gruppen Kommandeur of 1./JG-52. On 17 April I reached the 350 victory mark and on 8 May scored my last victory over a Yak 11. Hours later, the war was over and my Gruppe surrendered to the Americans in Pisek, Poland. In my two-and-a-half years of operations I had flown over 1,400 missions, 825 of which involved aerial combat, and had scored 352 victories.

Many German pilots experienced the novelty of fighting Americans in Soviet airspace. One of them explained the circumstances.

FRITZ LOSIGKEIT, LUFTWAFFE

When I became Kommodore of JG-51, I took advantage of one of
our few 'quiet' periods to train my Wing to intercept and attack
Allied bombers. We expected them to fly from England or Italy to
bomb Germany and then, due to the long distances involved, fly on
and land in Russia. We practised head-on attacks against our own
He177 four-engine bombers. One day, during a practice mission,
our ground crew announced the approach of a powerful force of
enemy bombers with fighter escort. I gathered my First and Third
Gruppen, which were already airborne, and ordered the Staff
Squadron to take off.

We soon overtook the bombers and lined up for a head-on
attack, as we had practised. As we did so, a large force of Mustangs
attacked from above, but we pressed home our attack, destroying
a single B-17 in the process. Heavy fighting followed, during which
a Mustang carried out an emergency landing on our airbase. When
the ground crews got to him, he was unfortunately dead, but the
map in his cockpit contained some useful information, which I
delivered to our Air Force command. As a result, we were ordered
to carry out a night attack on the airbases at Poltawa, where we
caught the Americans on the ground and destroyed 47 aircraft.

The major opponent remained the Russians and, however impressive
individual Soviet aces might be, the average Soviet pilot did not earn the
esteem of the Luftwaffe.

WALTER SCHUCK, LUFTWAFFE

On 17 June 1944, whilst stationed in Finland, my unit spotted
vapour trails in the sunlit midnight sky, which indicated a Russian
reconnaissance machine at about 25,000ft altitude. After 15 hours
of constant sorties, during which I had achieved 11 aerial victories, I
was naturally sleeping at the time, totally exhausted. However, after
only an hour's sleep, the alarm sounded and I was quickly running

for my aircraft to get airborne. It didn't seem to be a sortie with much hope of success, since we believed the Soviet aircraft to be a Spitfire and it had a substantial head start.

Once airborne, and with the vapour trails of the enemy machine standing out so clearly in the Arctic sky, all thoughts of tiredness left me as, together with my wingman, we concentrated on the task in hand. Slowly gaining on the Russian as we climbed, soon we, too, were making vapour trails, making it easy for our ground crews to watch our progress. However, the enemy pilot had not noticed our approach and, as we came within the last 2km of him, we could now see for sure that the Soviet-flown machine was definitely a Spitfire. Closing then to within 50m, I lined him up in my sights and paused for an instant, savouring the beauty of the moment. I then fired off my guns, hitting the fuselage and wings of the Spitfire, and it slowly began to spin, pulling out at about 18,000ft before spinning again. At about 12,000ft, a white dot separated from the crashing machine, indicating that the pilot had taken to his parachute. The burning machine then crashed into the Tundra.

When I landed, I was elated at this victory and was heartily congratulated by the ground crew. It was my 113th victory, my 12th in 24 hours and my first Spitfire.

Nevertheless, Germany was losing in the East as surely as on the other fronts. Numbers were always on the side of their opponents, although flying skills still won individual successes:

WALTER WOLFRUM, LUFTWAFFE

On the second day of the Soviet offensive against Lemburg, I took off, only to see over 100 bombers in the air, with as many accompanying fighters. My I Gruppe was the only German formation in the area and my squadron alone had lost four of its 14 aircraft during the previous day's fighting. My first two missions involved heavy fighting with large numbers of Il2s,

Yak9s and Airacobras, each time shooting down two Yaks. On my third mission, I shot down four from a group of 12 Laggs in only a few minutes. My fourth mission was against large formations of bombers, but I couldn't get through the fighter protection and, in trying, my wingman received a hit and was forced to depart. I then spotted large numbers of P-39 Airacobras at high altitude and climbed to 29,000ft to attack them. I engaged my first of these, but another latched on to my tail. Finishing off the one in front, I initiated a spin to escape my assailant, but felt a hit in my right hip which left me groggy. After spinning into cloud, I pulled out, then immediately blacked out. When I came out of the cloud, I was again attacked and could only escape by entering the next cloud, now feeling very weak and breathless. Flying lower to remove my oxygen mask, I was engaged by flak and was horrified to find I was flying eastwards, on the verge of blacking out. Fading rapidly, I gently turned westwards and flew as long as I could before lining myself up to land in a flat meadow in front of me. By astonishing luck, it was my own airfield and, lowering the flaps and the undercarriage, I landed the aircraft, then immediately passed out, my engine still running.

Luftwaffe pilots continued to fight until the final Russian offensive against Berlin in April and May 1945.

* * *

In the West, the war had not ended for fighter pilots with the defeat of the Luftwaffe's air offensive against Britain. The RAF continued to fly patrols, to dogfight with enemy aircraft and to mount raids. One target of their attentions was a trio of German warships trapped in the harbour at Brest. The escape of these vessels – the battleships *Scharnhorst* and *Gneisenau* and the cruiser *Prinz Eugen* – into the open sea, or their return home, would make a considerable impact on Germany's war effort. The RAF was determined to stop them, but suffered a great humiliation when, on 12 February 1942, all three broke out of harbour and made a run for it up the Channel to safety in German ports. An attack on the ships by torpedo-carrying Swordfish naval aircraft, all of which were shot down, is considered one of the bravest actions of the war.

LARRY ROBILLARD, RCAF

On the morning of 12 February 1942, I led a pair of Spitfires on a reconnaissance flight from Boulogne down the Channel to the south. The cloud was low – 500ft – but the visibility was reasonable enough when we were ordered to return to Gravesend, where the squadron was brought to cockpit readiness and scrambled just before noon.

I had no idea of where we were going or what we were looking for when I saw three old biplanes, carrying torpedoes, flying low towards the French coast. Amazed, I recognized them as Swordfish and noticed another three in the flight. They were so damned slow that we 'S' weaved to stay with them.

With a cloud base of about 1,600ft Johnnie Rutherford, an Australian, warned us of 18-plus bandits above. We turned into the attack and a strenuous running dogfight ensued as we tried desperately to protect the Swordfish. I saw a FW-190 with his wheels down to reduce his speed and I fired at a very wide, almost impossible angle; but before I could do much he blew up the Swordfish, whipped up his gear and disappeared into the cloud.

The dogfight, as usual, had fanned out over a wide area and I came out of cloud and looked right down the funnel of a German battleship, with others nearby and an escort of destroyers and E-boats.

The flak was intense so I made off very smartly, and had a running fight with more 109s before returning to Gravesend where, at the de-briefing, we learned for the first time that we had seen the epic escape of the German battle-cruisers, *Scharnhorst, Gneisenau* and *Prinz Eugen*. All the Swordfish were lost and their leader, Lieutenant Commander Esmonde, was posthumously awarded the VC.

BRIAN KINGCOME, RAF

All combats are much the same, and the only one I remember with any clarity was a fiasco. Captain Victor Beamish, CO of RAF Kenley, flying a 'rhubarb' [a section of two aircraft wave-hopping across the Channel under the radar screen to attack opportunity targets in France] observed three capital ships steaming up the Channel. He immediately reported them on his RT, but nobody took him seriously enough to initiate immediate action.

I was Commanding Officer of 72 Squadron at Gravesend, and three times we were called to cockpit standby and three times stood down. The fourth time we were briefed to rendezvous over Manston immediately with three other Spitfire squadrons and six naval Swordfish torpedo-carrying biplanes, who (we were told) were to attack some German E-boats, which were nothing more than fast, lightly armed launches.

We duly made contact with the Swordfish, but no Spitfires showed so the Swordfish headed east out to sea with us following in very poor visibility. E-boats were conspicuous by their absence, but I suddenly found myself sitting at about 200ft over a particularly beautiful battleship. I was mentally congratulating the Navy when she opened up at us with all guns. Even this didn't phase me since the Navy usually shot at us, but eventually it dawned that in fact I was looking at *Prinz Eugen*, in company with *Gneisenau* and *Scharnhorst*, the pride of the German Navy, making their famous Channel dash. The Swordfish were incredible. At 80 knots they flew straight and level, directly into the German guns. Shells were exploding all around them and knocking them into the sea, but still the remaining ones went steadily on. Then Me109s and the new FW-190s arrived in strength, and in the ensuing fracas the last of the Swordfish went down. The German fleet sailed on unscathed.

After we landed I asked my armourer to have my camera gun film (an innovation at that time) developed as soon as possible, as I hoped to have some shots of the new 190s and perhaps confirmation of one or two destroyed. 'Sorry, sir,' he told me later, 'afraid I forgot to take the cover off the lens.'

The ships' route up the Channel was protected by the Luftwaffe. The operation was planned meticulously and led by Germany's most well-known fighter pilot.

ADOLF GALLAND, LUFTWAFFE

In February 1942, I organized and conducted the fighter escort for the spectacular 'Channel Dash' – the breakout of the German battleships *Scharnhorst, Gneisenau* and *Prinz Eugen*, through the English Channel.

JOSEPH HAIBÖCK, LUFTWAFFE

Probably the toughest mission I ever went on was the close protection of the battle ships *Gneisenau* and *Scharnhorst* and the cruiser *Prinz Eugen* from Brest through the English Channel to Hamburg and Kiel. On 11 February 1942, all of the Gruppenkommandeure and Squadron Leaders serving in the West were ordered to Audembert, to the JG 26 Command Post. There, we were greeted by our former Kommodore, now General of Fighters Galland and were told our mission. The plan had been worked out to the minutest detail and security had been excellent.

On 11 February 1942, with the arrival of suitable weather, the decision to commence the operation was taken and, waiting at St Omer, we received the 'operation on' signal at 1700 hours. It was now time to brief the pilots. Every unit would take part. Sixteen machines were to fly either side of each ship. My Kommandeur took the French coast side and I took the English coast side. We took over from II Gruppe near Abbeville and were advised that we had not yet been discovered. Visibility was good, with the cloud base at 600 to 1,200ft. At 1115 hours, we handed over to III Gruppe and landed at St Omer at 1225. III Gruppe then had the first enemy contact and made a successful defence against torpedo-carrying aircraft. The deep flying deception missions and radio silence was cancelled. Deteriorating weather then delayed the handover to JG-2, so JG-26 had to continue to help out. II Gruppe relieved III Gruppe, and at 1530, we were once again on our way, reaching the convoy north of Dunkirk. I remember spotting twin-engined aircraft that quickly disappeared into the clouds, then we were attacked by a unit of Hurricanes, which we forced away. When our time came to leave, the clouds had sunk very low and it had started to snow. We were therefore relieved when we once again reached the French coast. At the coast, a *Schwarm* from JG-2 'Richthofen' joined us and together we flew to a Belgian forward airbase, where we landed in driving snow and immediately took on fuel and prepared for the next phase. However, the unit we were to relieve had not managed to reach its operational area due to the weather and, as the snow grew thicker, the operation was called off. We were told that the weather had become so bad that the enemy would not be able to take off either. The following morning we were told that, with the help of the weather, the mission had been a success.

Encounters with enemy fighters and attacks on shipping kept the RAF busy in the Channel.

BUD MALLOY, RCAF

In June 1942, I first met the great Irish fighter pilot, Wing Commander 'Paddy' Finucane, when he was leading the Redhill Wing. The day he went missing, ten of us managed to get airborne and three rescue boats were involved in the search. By the time we arrived in the area one boat had been sunk, one was on fire and the third was picking up the survivors of the other two. We, of course, were sure that Paddy was aboard the remaining boat. We had no sooner taken up position when 20-plus FW-190s were reported and attacked. This engagement was probably the longest between fighter aircraft since the Battle of Britain. It lasted 25 minutes from the first attack to the last. We were relieved by another squadron and the rescue boat returned to port without further incident. Unfortunately Paddy had not survived his attempt to ditch his Spitfire and the RAF lost its leading fighter pilot.

The next significant event was the landing of troops at Dieppe in Normandy. This was a fiasco, though Allied planners were to claim its lessons had been valuable in the planning of D-Day. For some pilots it was their first crack at the enemy.

JACKIE RAE, RCAF

My first real contact with enemy fighters came on 19 August 1942, when the Squadron took part in the ill-fated landing at Dieppe. The day before, we flew to Hawkinge, near Dover, and were briefed on what was the most important amphibious operation up to that time. Our job was to keep the Luftwaffe off the backs of our brother Canadian soldiers below. On that day the Squadron flew four missions, but our most exciting was during the withdrawal of the ground forces when our formation was very heavily engaged and Lloyd Chadburn fought a brilliant action without loss. As our Spitfires approached the battered convoy of ships to commence our protective patrol formation, 15 FW-190s dived on us from astern. Chadburn brought the squadron round in a very tight turn and reversed the tables so effectively that three of the 190s were destroyed. Hurriedly reforming, we resumed our cover over the ships when seven Ju88s appeared. 'Chad' attacked head-on and we damaged six enemy bombers before they withdrew.

DS GENTILE, RAF

My first two victories were over Dieppe while flying with the 133 Eagle Squadron.

The FW-190, which I got in this occasion, had just finished shooting down one of the Spitfires when I jumped him. He started to roll for the deck immediately and I followed him, clobbering the FW-190 at about 3,000ft, at which time he rolled over lazily and slowly and hit the beach where the Commandos were coming in.

After I had gotten the FW, a Ju88 started to dive-bomb the troops on the ground. I managed to get on his tail and started to clobber him. The Ju88 jettisoned its bombs in the Channel and missed its target. I closed in and got one engine burning. The aircraft finally exploded and crashed inland.

DUNCAN SMITH, RAF

At the time of combat I didn't think too much about my feelings, but upon returning home and being relaxed you can look back on all the things you did and didn't do and see the reason behind each move.

Robert Lea's voice crackled on the RT '. . . Vaxine Leader, 20-plus bandits approaching Abbeville, Angles 17 . . .' Patrolling as part of the Dieppe raid, August 1942, I led the Squadron down in a steep dive from 23,000ft. Clipping a big cloudbank I came up behind one of them and hammered a good burst into his port engine and wing root at very close range. Large pieces flew off the wing, and one engine caught fire. His gunner kept shooting at me with great accuracy. Tracer whizzed over my cockpit but I was determined to get him and fired again into the cockpit area. Suddenly, four big thuds as cannon shells rocked my Spitfire; a bang below the throttle quadrant, a sharp pain in my left leg, and flames in the cockpit. I baled out just in time. After half an hour, an RN motor launch plucked me out of the Channel and confirmed they had seen the Dornier crash into the sea. Back at Hornchurch the next day I heard the Wing had been destroyed – one probable, and fourteen damaged for the loss of three pilots and four aircraft. My Squadron accounting for five destroyed and four damaged.

By this stage in the war, Fighter Command was becoming increasingly committed to its role as bomber escort.

BUD MALLOY, RCAF

On August 24 1942, we escorted 12 B-17s to Le Tait and, although the controller warned that 40-plus bandits were nearby, the trip was uneventful until we had seen our bombers safely on their way home and turned back into France.

Suddenly we saw two 190s diving below our squadron. The CO went down on the two enemy aircraft with two sections of four Spitfires, leaving me as top cover with another Spitfire. The two 190s were obviously the bait as the remainder of the 40-plus, previously reported, poured down out of the sun. As I warned my CO, I turned my pair directly into the attack and my head-on approach forced a 190 to pull up sharply. I could see exactly what was going to happen – he ran out of power in his near vertical climb and gave me a no-deflection shot as he stalled out. Although in the ensuing dogfight we were reportedly out-numbered by ten to one, we shot down four and lost one of our pilots. It was a rather interesting few minutes.

Their counterparts in the US Army Air Force were involved in many of the same tasks.

JIM GOODSON, RAF/USAAF

On 16 August 1943, 170 B-17 Flying Fortresses took off to bomb Le Bourget, the main Paris airport; a short mission for us. The bombers were to be escorted at 23,000ft, by four Thunderbolt Groups [192 fighters], with Spitfires sweeping the area at 15,000ft.

Before we joined up with the bombers, we saw 30-plus enemy

fighters coming up from behind. Don Blakeslee, Colonel commanding the Group, asked me to cover him and took his flight into the attack. The FW-190s broke away and we followed in a vertical dive, reaching such speed that we not only left our wingmen behind, but also caught up with the 190s.

Blakeslee was getting hits on one of them, but we were now in the hornet's nest and three 190s curved in behind him. Due to my speed, I was able to shoot one of them down. We were now below 10,000ft and fighting for our lives in the kind of dogfight where, every time we attacked, we had to break off because we were attacked ourselves.

I was able to shoot down another 190 off Blakeslee's tail, but not before his Thunderbolt was badly hit. I was able to drive off other 190s by pressing home attacks, although by now I was out of ammunition. Although both he and the plane were covered in oil, I managed to guide him back to an emergency landing at Manston. The Thunderbolt had over 20 cannon holes, including one which took out a cylinder in the engine.

Fighter sweeps, however, still went on . . .

ANDY MACKENZIE, RCAF

On 20 December 1943, I was flying number two to the Wing Leader. We were on a fighter sweep when I reported a gaggle of Huns flying south, which put us on intersecting courses and soon we arrived at the ideal position for a quarter attack. I could not understand why the leader did not take the whole wing down, and since I could not control my youthful exuberance any longer, I broke formation, slipped under the enemy aeroplanes and destroyed two FW-190s with the rest of the boys looking on. Then the whole wing attacked and there was a tremendously large dogfight.

I found myself alone, so I decided to climb up through the cloud in an attempt to find my Wing Leader, whom I had left unguarded;

but as I broke cloud there was a 109 dead ahead of me. I fired, hit him in the cockpit, and he turned and dived straight for the ground.

Eventually, I found the Wing Leader and was able to give him some protection on the way home, but I knew that I had broken a cardinal rule. Had I not downed three enemy fighters I would have been turfed off the wing and sent back to Canada in disgrace because a number two just does not leave his leader. However, all was forgiven because a short time later I was awarded an immediate DFC.

. . . and one of them gave this Canadian pilot an exhilarating introduction to combat:

HART FINLEY, RCAF

My first encounter with an enemy aircraft occurred on 30 December, 1943, while on a Ramrod mission. My log-book reads: 'Sweep to pick up 500-odd Forts and Libs. Spotted four Me109s and bounced them with Claude Weaver. Each got one destroyed. Saw them crash.' Our wing was at 25,000ft when I reported four aircraft cruising a few thousand feet above ground level. I was jolted out of my complacent state when our 'Wingco', Hugh Godefroy, ordered 'Go get 'em.'

I allowed our speed to get much too high in the dive and realized, as we rapidly closed on the 109s, that even with throttle fully retarded we were going to overshoot and give away our presence and most likely our advantage as well. We ended up line-abreast of the formation, one on each side. Those big, black Nazi crosses looked rather menacing to the uninitiated. Suddenly the formation split, two to starboard and two to port. I, being on the left flank, turned into the pair breaking in my direction, lined up on the nearer of the two and blasted it from about 200 yards. It straightened out, dropped its nose and headed for the ground while I gave another short burst of cannon fire. The aircraft smoked noticeably, went out of control and plunged to the ground. I never saw the second aircraft after the initial break, so executed a rapid, spiralling climb to 20,000ft, looking out for any sign of Claude, who radioed he had scored a victory and was also climbing away. There was no doubt in my mind that had I been less impetuous on the initial attack we could have bagged all four, considering the tactical advantage we had.

Raids and patrols were not the RAF's only tasks at this time. One crew had to deliver equipment to the Maquis.

ROBERT EDWARD MACKETT, RCAF

While other clandestine activities were flown from Tempsford, we were charged to fly singly and to deliver three to six containers, each weighing about 300lb packed with arms, ammunitions, explosives, wireless equipment, food, etc, and anything to hamper the enemy. These containers had to be delivered to a small reception committee waiting in a farmer's field (or woods) somewhere in France or Belgium and dropped by parachute from a height of 450–1000ft. The major challenge was to locate this small group of patriots who identified themselves on the ground with three red hand-torches and one white torch flashing a coded signal. My navigator and I selected our route to the drop area and to avoid detection and plotting by the enemy we flew about 500ft above the ground. Over the continent, flying at 180mph, the principal navigation was by map reading from a ¼in map handled by the bomb-aimer in the front turret with a running patter to the navigator. On foggy or hazy nights flying 'up moon' the pinpoints were reported by the rear gunner, looking 'down moon'. Locating the reception committee was sometimes very difficult since they were attempting to conceal themselves from searching Germans. Often they placed themselves on the side of a hill or in a small clearing in the forest. The drop itself was done at 450–500ft at 125mph. For the safety of the reception committee, it was important to discover the drop areas, place the load on the site and leave quickly to avoid drawing attention to the operation. Such operations took alert flying and very accurate navigation. During the dark period when 161 Squadron stood down, we went back to 214 Squadron at Chedburgh, resuming conventional bombing and mining trips.

As the Allied effort increased in intensity, the Luftwaffe felt the strain.

ADOLF GALLAND, LUFTWAFFE

In 1943 I was given the responsibility for Fighter Operations in Sicily, just before the Allied landings. But, with the Allied air superiority established, this was an impossible task. I then moved on to concentrate my efforts on the air defence in Germany. RAF Bomber Command was operating large forces by night. Meanwhile, the American 8th Air Force was flying missions out of England every day. I was given responsibility for the Night Fighter Arm, too, and was, in the same rhythm as the war, working 24 hours every day. The RAF and USAAF steadily gained air superiority during a time when greater fighter protection was badly needed. However, by the time this was achieved, fuel shortages – due to the incessant air attacks – became our problem. I never succeeded in convincing Hitler to concentrate the entire effort on air defence, and even when the advanced Me262 jet became available, my efforts to use this purely in a fighter role were strictly refused by Hitler. The war had already been lost years previously and the earlier introduction of the jet fighters would not have changed its course. Even if we had prevented the day offensive of the USAAF, the war would simply have been prolonged, allowing Russia to occupy even more German territory. By the end of 1944, I was discharged from my position and ordered to set up an Me262 fighter unit. Thus, I started the war as an Oberleutnant leading a squadron, and ended it as a Generalleutnant leading a squadron.

The major event of the war in Europe was the Allied invasion of Normandy in June 1944. The date was kept highly secret and was changed, owing to adverse weather, from the 5 to the 6 of June. A Mosquito pilot was ordered to deliver the news.

MOOSE FUMERTON, RCAF

On 4 June 1944, I flew to 10 Group Headquarters to pick up some brown paper envelopes for delivery to several aerodromes in south-west England. Delivery was temporarily postponed however, but on 5 June I was given the go-ahead. At each aerodrome a motorcycle pulled up alongside the Mosquito shortly after it touched down, and without shutting off the engines an envelope was handed out and the motorcycle sped away. I looked at the weather and shook my head. In the small hours of 6 June I flew over to take a surreptitious peek at the beachheads. It reminded me of the scene in the old western movies where the scout stopped and said, 'It's too quiet.' Quite so, all hell was about to break loose.

Another Canadian flyer saw the invasion itself.

RICHARD ROHMER, RCAF

As with all other combat units, the pace of our activity accelerated in the late spring of '44 as we moved towards D-Day, 6 June. On that day I had the enviable opportunity to be doing a low-level recce up and down the British and Canadian beaches at H-Hour. Cloud forced my leader and I down to 500ft, from which we had a magnificent panoramic view of the troops pouring out of the landing craft on to the beaches, and in the smoke-covered horizon out to sea the wake of approaching vessels, and beyond them the winking flashes of the hundreds of naval guns firing at enemy targets – right under us. I had the best seat in the house.

Airmen protected the invasion fleet and supported the troops once they were ashore, braving flak, armour and small-arms fire as they flew at low altitude over the battlefield.

HARRY J DOWDING, RCAF

On 8 June, while dive-bombing tanks in Caen, I was shot by flak, which pierced the gas tank and promptly sprayed gasoline all over me. While I was trying to decide how to bail out without becoming a flaming torch, I spotted a freshly bulldozed landing strip, just above the beach. In order to avoid sparks, I left all switches on, put the wheels down and went in for a normal landing on the soft earth. All went well until near the end of my landing run when a French farmer with a horse-drawn load of hay tried to beat me across the landing strip. It finished in a tie. Result – one French horse destroyed, one French farmer damaged. Miraculously no fire, and I walked away unhurt. I made my way to the beach and returned to England that night on a motor torpedo boat in a 50-mile per hour gale. I was seasick the whole way, much to the amusement of the British Navy, some of whom eventually joined me at the rail.

On 27 June, 1944, we were flying an armed reconnaissance east of Caen when Larry Robillard spotted six Me109s low-flying towards our lines near Caen. I led my flight to the attack and, as we got closer, I could see they were carrying what appeared to be 500lb bombs. As we bored in, they saw us and dropped the bombs and took evasive action. During the next several minutes I shot down two in flames; one pilot managed to bail out. Stan McClarty shot down two, one of which blew up, scorching his aircraft. Larry Robillard's guns jammed and the other two got away. Terrible disappointment for Larry.

An urgent mission for the RAF was to put an end to the danger posed by Hitler's 'V' weapons – weapons of terror that had little strategical value. Fighters and bombers were dispatched to destroy their launch sites or deflect and intercept any of the long-range missiles already on the way.

RUSS BANNOCK, RCAF

On the night of 12 June 1944, the first V1s – also called 'buzz bombs' and 'doodle bugs' – first made their appearance over southern England. Although as a tactical weapon the buzz bomb had little value because of its inaccuracy, it was a means of intimidating the populus and thousands, who, with stoical fortitude, withstood the blitz of 1940. [The public] found themselves attacked by a weapon they could not understand – a bomb which, striking upon the ground, made little or no crater, but striking a building reduced it to rubble. Consequently, the squadron spent a month on patrols over the Channel against these dreaded flying bombs and during this period we shot down 83 flying bombs, all at night, and I was credited with 19 victories and accounted for four in one night sortie.

On 14 June 1944, I carried out a night intruder patrol, together with Bob Bruce as my navigator, to the airfields at Bourges and Avord, south-east of Paris. About midnight the airfield lights came on at Avord, so we kept a lookout for aircraft near the downwind leg of the airfield. We spotted some engine exhausts passing overhead but soon lost the aircraft silhouette on the base leg of the circuit. However, we soon noticed a flashing tail-light on the approach leg and started to attack. The airfield defences were obviously alerted and we were subjected to intense AA fire, causing us to break away from the airfield. Fortunately for us, the aircraft switched on his landing lights just prior to touchdown, so we made a beam attack, causing it to explode on the runway. In the light, we made out the shape of an Me110. We were again subject to intense AA fire over the airfield but managed to escape unscathed.

Now that pilots were taking part in front line fighting on the Continent they could find themselves pursuing targets that were highly intriguing.

RICHARD ROHMER, RCAF

On 17 July 1944, I was leading a section of four Mustangs on a tactical recce to the east of Caen in the Lisieux, Livarot sector. Heading south past Livarot I saw a huge staff car ahead going in the same direction. Its top was down. I could see that the vehicle was filled with what I believed to be brass. To my great regret I was prevented by order from attacking this superb (or any other) target of opportunity. Instead I was obliged to call 'Kenway', 83 Group Control Centre, and reported the target. As a result of my report, five miles later, the staff car was shot up by two Spits or Typhoons (identity not discovered to this day – Squadron Leader Lerous, later credited, was not airborne at the time). The damaged staff car hit a tree. It's important occupant was critically injured and out of the war. He was Field Marshal Erwin Rommel.

DON LAUBMAN, RCAF

Soon after D-Day we moved to Bény-sur-Mer, in Normandy, and on 2 July, when escorting some Mustangs, we ran into a gaggle of enemy fighters. I got two 190s in quick succession and two more were destroyed by other Falcon pilots, but we lost Bud Bowker, an able and experienced pilot with at least five victories. Our operations during August were highlighted by the terrible destruction we inflicted, by low-level strafing on enemy columns of trucks, staff cars, armoured cars, tanks and troop carriers as they fled from the Falaise pocket. This constant, relentless hammering by hundreds of our fighter bombers reached its climax on 18 August, when, from first light to nightfall, our Spitfires were almost continually over the road running eastward from Falaise and Argentan to the Seine.

At midday, fighter-reconnaissance pilots reported many roads jammed with vehicles; Dean Dover and his wingman reported 1,000–1,500 vehicles, jammed bumper to bumper, in a large wood near Argentan. Every serviceable Spitfire was put into the air. No attempt was made to fly large formations. Two, four or six Spitfires would go out together, dive and fire until all our ammunition was gone and then return for more. Throughout this long day, Spitfires and Typhoons blasted the enemy and destroyed thousands of transports. In my opinion 18 August 1944, ranks as one of the most important milestones in World War II.

Although the Germans were in retreat from Normandy, it could still be extremely dangerous for a flyer to be shot down there.

FREDDY EVANS, RCAF

We knocked off the lead elements [of the German forces] and for days destroyed everything in sight. An eventful day and unusual to have to return to base and re-arm rather than re-fuel. The history books show that a great part of the German Army escaped through the Gap but we know they didn't take most of their transport with them.

Although I saw few enemy aeroplanes airborne again, we encountered him on the ground and pounded him with cannon and bombs all the way to B154 in Germany. Finally word came down to cease destroying trains and motor transport as we would soon need them for our own use.

The squadron was airborne on a sortie at medium altitude when I reported two 190s below at nine o'clock going to three. A 90-degree turn to starboard and Danny Browne was on one and I had the other. It was too easy. I fired a short burst at long range and observed hits on the wing roots and tail, but the 190 took no evasive action. I closed steadily, fired another short burst and had good hits, but still he took no evasive action whatsoever. Curiosity or stupidity overcame me, so I flew up beside him to see what his problem was. His head was slumped forward on his chest, the 190 was in a steepening dive and his problem appeared to be that he was dead or would be in a very few seconds. Mesmerized, I followed

him for a bit, then pulled up and looked over my shoulder to see
two black pillars of smoke. While this was happening, my friend,
Ed Smith, was preparing for a forced landing with a dead engine.

I learned years later that the Germans who picked Ed up had
witnessed the downing of the 190s and only by proving that his guns
had not been fired, and thus was not a part of it, was he allowed to
become a POW.

Downed pilots found the French Resistance as much of a godsend as they
had always been.

GERALD BROWN, USAAF

I got in several scares, but was never able to bag one. The only real
interesting thing that happened to me was that I had to bail out of
a Mustang on 5 September 1944, due to engine failure. The French
Underground picked me up and I was back in England the same day.

As summer turned to autumn, fighter pilots fought on across France and
into the Netherlands.

BILL BANKS, RCAF

The Germans were pulling out of France and we began the great
adventurous trek following and supporting our victorious armies
as they pressed on through Belgium and Holland, only to be halted
in the fall of 1944 by the enemy's resistance at Arnhem. During one
dive-bombing sortie, I saw a motorcycle dispatch-rider on the road
and peeled-off to attack. The rider decided to beat it out to the
safety of a group of buildings. My strikes all fell behind him, but,
pulling up and away I saw the motorcycle and rider slithering across
the courtyard. I hope he is alive today.

Whenever the weather permitted, [the Germans] flew over the
battle area and we ranged far to the south to cut them off before
they could attack our ground troops. They generally operated

in small formations – rarely of more than a dozen aircraft – and generally we flew in about the same strength.

On another occasion our section of four Spitfires fought some 109s with some success. During the debriefing each of us was asked what we got. A dry Texan in our group replied: 'I got back!'

On 27 December 1944, the Squadron took off to sweep the Münster area and over the Rhine, I was surprised to see a 109 circling the airfield preparing to land. I engaged the 109 right over the airfield and during the ensuing melee I received a hit from ground fire which blew off one blade of my four-bladed propeller. The resulting vibration was enormous, the radio was shattered and all instruments read maximum. I was barely able to stay airborne but somehow managed to make the 30 minutes back to base. The 109 escaped.

ART SAGER, RCAF

The clear, hot days of August were the busiest in terms of operational flights; elements of the wing being in the air three or more times a day. The soft-bellied Spitfire was not designed for ground-strafing and dive-bombing, but for a period these were its exclusive tasks in trying to prevent the escape of the enemy with his armour from Normandy.

In the early afternoon of 27 September 1944, I was leading 416 Squadron on a patrol east of Nijmegen. Suddenly we spotted 50-plus aircraft below us at low-level. They were flying west in fairly close formation. Diving in a spiral, we made a near-perfect bounce on what turned out to be bomb-carrying FW-190s and Me109s.

From 50 yards distance, I fired at the number two of a gaggle of Me109s. He exploded. When the debris cleared, I broke sharp port behind the leader, fired from even closer and his aircraft also exploded in a mass of yellow flame and debris.

The dogfight lasted minutes only, but the Squadron destroyed six of the enemy and seriously damaged three without loss. Equally satisfying was the dispersal of the attack on our ground forces, the enemy apparently thinking he had been set upon by a Wing rather than a Squadron of Spitfires.

Some fighter pilots, now able to cover vast distances in their long-range aircraft, found themselves as far afield as eastern Germany.

ROBIN OLDS, USAAF

I had still to experience my first actual aerial combat, an event which took place early on the morning of 13 August [1944], somewhere close to Montmirail in France. This involved a surprise attack I was able to pull off when jumping two FW-190s down at ground level. After a brief but hectic flight I was able to down both of them. Things moved faster after that. Just a couple of weeks later my wingman and I attacked a group of Messerschmitt 109s – there were between 55 and 60 of them – and had a heck of a fight. The 109s were headed for the bomber stream. The engagement began at 28,000ft over the Muritz Zee and, in the usual fashion for such affairs, finished down on the deck. By then, we were close to Rostock on the Baltic. During the battle, I was able to bag three 109s while my wingman was responsible for two destroyed. But what I remember most from this was the trip home. It was long, slow and cold, my canopy having been shot away. Things worked out however, and this – only my second combat – resulted in the award of the Silver Star.

It was at this time that Germany introduced an aircraft that could have changed the course of the war. The Me262 was the world's first jet fighter. Had Hitler allowed its widespread deployment in aerial combat it could have wreaked terrible destruction among the Allied bomber fleets. His hesitation to do this – he wanted it to be developed as a bomber – meant that too few of them were available and that they appeared too late to have a significant impact.

HERMANN BUCHNER, LUFTWAFFE

On 26 November 1944, I made my first operational sortie in a Me262, 'Yellow 8'. The weather was not easy, with a huge cloud bank to the west. At 1100 hours, I received the order to take off and, with the alert siren roaring, I started my jet power plants, which ran smoothly, and taxied to the end of the runway. I was to intercept a reconnaissance aircraft in the Munich area.

After taking off and raising my undercarriage, I carefully checked over the instruments, especially the engine temperature gauges, tuned the radio for the radar control station 'Bavaria' and called in. In a split second, a voice identified itself and ordered me to steer a course of 340 degrees at altitude 7,000m for a target at a distance of 20km. My Me262 quickly reached this altitude and I armed the weapons and checked my instruments, ready for action. Unfortunately, despite two attempts, I never found the target and it got away.

I was then given a new course to steer and was soon under the control of a Stuttgart area radar station named 'Leander'. This was approximately over Augsburg, I followed a cloud bank eastwards, alone above the clouds, blue sky above and vapour trails behind me.

'Leander' called me again – target 70km, course 270, height 8,000m. My Me262 shot towards it, engines running normally. At 10km range I could make out a small spot, but as it slowly grew, I identified an American P-38 Lightning returning to France. Grasping the weapon handle, I fired the first projectile, which passed over the top of its target. The second was accurate and hit the Lightning in the fuselage, my Me262 soon shooting past it. The Lightning then went into a spin and was soon immersed, burning, in the clouds. The pilot, Lieutenant Irvin J Rickey, got out safely and became a POW in Germany. He was the first pilot to be shot down by a jet aircraft.

WALTER SCHUCK, LUFTWAFFE

November and December of 1944, I spent in Germany, returning to northern Norway in January 1945 for a short time. From there I led my Squadron against incoming British aircraft, where I was able to score a few more victories. Shortly afterwards, I was trained in JG-7 on the Me262 and then, on 24 March 1945, I was appointed Squadron Leader of 3./JG-7.

Flying the Me262 in combat was a totally new experience, which initially took a lot of getting used to. With the very high speed of this aircraft, closing speeds, particularly with frontal attacks, were much higher, giving less time to attack. Also, the high combat speeds left wingmen scattered all over the sky and because of this, some of my jet victory claims were unconfirmed for the lack of a witness. However, flying the Me262, I was credited with a further eight victories, including four B-17s. By the end of April 1945, I was shot down myself by American fighters and was forced to use my parachute.

By the beginning of 1945 the Mosquito had become the most useful Allied bomber, and was the aircraft most hated by the enemy – Joseph Goebbels' diaries testify to his apoplectic rage at the damage done on their nightly visits to Berlin. A pilot who flew one recalls his final combat:

RED SOMERVILLE, RCAF

The most memorable combat I had was on the night of January 23–24 1945, in a Mosquito Type XIII.

For one thing it was the last combat I had and for another it was the most fascinating. We were vectored all over the sky at heights from 2,500ft to 5,000ft and passed from one GCI to another without any joy. Finally, we were getting low on fuel when I noticed anti-aircraft bursts off my left wing at range about three miles. Just then three searchlights provided me with a beautiful intersection and visual of an aircraft. I

immediately turned in that direction and my navigator picked
up a contact, which turned out to be a Ju88. I closed to 200ft
and opened fire. The aircraft caught fire and crashed three
miles west of Diest.

Another flyer had a very different experience in his last combat, finding
himself a POW less than a month before the end of the war.

DON LAUBMAN, RCAF

On 14 April 1945, I was leading my squadron on an armed
reconnaissance north of Bremen. I spotted two trucks travelling
down a dirt road and kicking up a cloud of dust in the process. I
commenced a strafing attack and lined-up on the rear vehicle.
I noticed strikes from the four 20mm cannon and some flames.
Then I pulled through to the lead vehicle and commenced firing.
However, just as I was passing over the first truck, it exploded in
a huge sheet of flame that engulfed my aircraft.

Apparently it was a gasoline tanker. As I came through the
conflagration, I saw that my aircraft had turned jet black. I was able
to climb to about 7,000ft but noticed that the coolant temperature
was going off the clock. At that time the Weser River was the
demarcation line between the rival forces. I could see the river in
the distance and tried desperately to reach it. However, my engine
first failed and then caught fire which sealed my fate. I was forced to
bail out at about 800ft, five miles short of the river. After bouncing
off the tailplane on the way out, I was soon apprehended by the
German Army.

His colleagues, meanwhile, continued to score heavily against the
Luftwaffe.

CHRIS FOXLEY-NORRIS, RAF

On 22 April 1945, I led the Banff Mosquito Wing on an anti-shipping strike into the Kattegat, which proved abortive owing to fog. While returning across the North Sea we encountered a German anti-force of 18 Ju88s and Heinkel 111s. In spite of continuing low cloud and poor visibility, we shot down nine aircraft confirmed and one probable. Unusually, post-war research indicated that 15 German aircraft failed to return to base. This must have been one of the most comprehensive single-action defeats inflicted on Luftwaffe operational aircraft.

Although the conflict was all but over, German forces continued to fight with spirit and energy both on land and in the air. For this pilot, the most exciting moments of the war were also the last:

HART FINLEY, RCAF

On 2 May 1945, I led a flight to strafe a German airfield and we left a number of enemy aircraft burning on the ground. Returning to base we intercepted a Ju88 at 2,500ft which went into a steep dive. Before it reached ground level I got in a burst of cannon fire and saw several strikes. Suddenly, it went into a tight turn, but I was able to score more hits, whereupon it straightened out, slowed and plunged into the deck.

As I pulled away, I was jolted by a loud bang, followed by flame entering the cockpit. In bailng out, my right foot got jammed between the seat and the fuselage, but with the strong urge to survive (shot of adrenaline) I broke free and the parachute opened. As I hit the ground I saw a horde of Germans heading in my direction. I sped across the rising ground towards a wooded area and heard a burst of rifle shots 'zinging' around my head; but I managed to get away and hid until darkness and then made my way south-westerly towards our advancing forces. Without my right boot, which was still in my Spitfire, I managed to walk about 20 miles before dawn and, that afternoon, was picked up by a British tank and sent to a hospital in Lauenberg, where minor shrapnel wounds and light burns were treated. The following morning an Auster returned me to my base and the end of the war was announced the next morning.

5

THE PACIFIC WAR

Statistically, the air war against Japan was a smaller conflict than that in Europe. Fewer planes and pilots were involved, fewer sorties flown, smaller tonnages of bombs were dropped, and less people died. Nevertheless, aircraft were of overwhelming importance. The war began and ended in the air, and in the period between the attack on Pearl Harbor in December 1941 and the dropping of the atom bombs in August 1945, it was Japan's aircraft that ensured her dominance over the Pacific and America's that caused her to lose it. Though British and Commonwealth pilots were active in India and Burma, it was the United States that bore the greatest burden and, though the US Army Air Force provided the B-17s and B-29s that bombed Japan's cities, it was the carrier-launched, naval fighter-bombers that wrested victory from their counterparts of the Imperial Japanese Navy. Even the US Army Air Force B-25 bombers that made the innovative, long-range 'Doolittle Raids' against Japan in April 1942 did so courtesy of the Navy, for they flew from the carrier USS *Hornet*.

It is often imagined that the start of the Pacific war – the raid on Pearl Harbor – came as a complete surprise to the American government and the US Navy. While the attack itself was indeed a bolt from the blue because the two nations were not officially at war, every sailor in the Fleet was aware that conflict could break out at any moment, and that all of America's Pacific bases were potential targets. In Hawaii military installations were therefore guarded against saboteurs, patrolling aircraft were fully armed, and an exercise – a simulated air-raid on Pearl Harbor – was carried out less than 48 hours before the real one. A Navy flyer later commented:

THOMAS H MOORER, US NAVY

Some books about the Pacific war make it seem that all of us were oblivious to the fact that the Japanese existed. In fact, there was a tremendous amount of concern about them and we were fairly certain there was going to be a war. The only questions were when and how it would start. We (a PBY squadron) were carrying bombs all the time. [Admiral] Halsey was ready to go to war right then and there. That's how tense things were by early December.

This concern was not misplaced. The Japanese Navy had studied Pearl Harbor for years and trained its pilots for months. On 7 December, the attacking force arrived over its target a few minutes before eight o'clock. The nine-year-old daughter of a Marine officer, seeing the bursts of anti-aircraft shells, rushed outside to see what was happening:

JOAN ZUBER

Then, suddenly, out of the corner of my eye I saw a grayish-black column of smoke. Something was burning. I dropped the book and ran out the door to look.

Fire! There! Over the bushes toward Luke Field I saw fire! Smoke and flames rose, filling the sky with a black cloud. It looked like the water tower was on fire! How could the water tower be on fire? It was made of metal! 'Run!' my brain ordered. 'Run back inside the quarters. Tell Mother.'

I ran out the front door to see what was causing the puffs of smoke. Just then a strange plane with red balls on the sides of its body swooped low over my head, diving towards the masts of the *West Virginia* and *Tennessee*. What plane was that? What was it doing flying so low?

In a nearby barracks one member of a patrol-bomber crew was jolted into reality:

DONALD PATRICK FINN, US NAVY

I was seated on the edge of my bunk trying to decide whether I should shave before going to mass when the high pitched whine of an airplane engine pulling its freight out of a dive forced itself upon my consciousness.

Then there was an explosion as of a charge of dynamite being set off. The two sounds seemed to have some connection. Everyone crowded to the windows and looked out. There was a cloud of black smoke and flying dirt between the edges of the buildings . . . followed by another explosion and the sight of a low wing monoplane pulling out of a dive and standing almost on its tail. It was awfully close to the ground.

For the space of a couple of deep breaths there was silence and then somebody said, 'The yellow bastards.' Then everybody began talking at once, grabbing clothes and getting into them. 'How in the hell did they get in here and where the hell did they come from?' Everybody was asking everybody else.

I said to Van Brocklin who was cursing the Japs heartily, 'Well, it looks like the real thing' and he answered 'Yeah, and I'm glad of it, now we can give them sons of bitches what they have been asking for.' It's funny but no one seemed to be frightened, though by now several bombs had fallen and the barracks trembled slightly. Several guys raced downstairs to look out over the sick bay and the harbor from the main entrance. Now and then from the windows where a few foolish ones watched came a cheer as a Jap plane fell smoking into the bay.

Belatedly, I thought of rushing down to the hanger, sure of the sight that would greet the eye. There were many of us taking advantage of the lull in the bombing that came now. We poured out of the exits, being careful not to bunch up, and began legging it for the hangers, glancing frequently upward in the direction of possible strafers. But there were none. There was no danger to be seen until one got to the paint-stripping shop. In front of it was a bomb crater and concrete and glass scattered about for an area of 50 yards. All the windows were blown out. That was the first bomb destruction I had ever seen, and it was impressive.

Our hanger was ablaze, its windows mostly in pieces on the ramp. VP-22's ramp had been hit harder than any other Squadron. Only two planes out of twelve weren't damaged, damage ranging all the way from complete demolition to a punctured oil tank and bullet holes in the wings . . .

One of his officers was already outdoors when the attack began:

THOMAS H MOORER, US NAVY

I got dressed and was leaving for the naval base with my co-pilot when we saw the Japanese planes. We rushed as hard as we could and arrived at the base while the first wave was striking Hickam Field and Pearl Harbor. We had twelve planes, which were parked outside the hangers, and most of them were shot up quite severely. Virtually all the damage was done by strafing, because there was no bombing of any significance on the island itself.

I had a grandstand view of the attack. I saw both the *Pennsylvania* and the *Nevada* get hit, and I saw the *Arizona* go up in a tremendous explosion. I also had a good view of Japanese planes falling. This came mainly during the second attack wave, by which time the defences and ships gun crews had gotten organized. A good many Japanese planes were shot down by antiaircraft fire . . .

Another naval flyer saw an enemy plane come to grief nearby:

ARTHUR W PRICE JR, US NAVY

A Zero fighter came down. We thought he was going to strafe us because his guns were going, but evidently the pilot had been shot already. He just flew straight into the ground, shooting the whole way. He hit the ground maybe 500 feet from us and was thrown out of the plane. He was dead of course, and all chopped up, so we threw him in the back of the truck.

At least one Japanese pilot seems to have been killed after crash-landing. The nine-year-old witness recalled that, as her family emerged from shelter after the raid:

JOAN ZUBER

A Marine walked by. 'Do you want to see the dead Jap pilot out front?' he asked. 'His plane crashed in the harbor and they pulled his body up to the grass.'

The pilot was lying in the grass fifty feet in front of [our quarters]. His arms were flung out, his face turned to the side. I scanned his body searching for his wound. I couldn't find it. Peggy gestured with her finger, pointing to a splotch of blood on his chest where, according to the Marine, he had been bayoneted in the heart. The enemy lay amidst the exploded pieces of the *Arizona*. Metal, glass, forks, knives, and plate decking were his final resting place . . .

The Japanese pilots, who had trained extensively for the operation, had assumed that by the time of their arrival over Hawaii the declaration of war would have been received. Veterans were therefore horrified to find later that their mission was considered a 'sneak attack'. Expecting the Americans to be aware of the outbreak of hostilities, the Japanese also anticipated higher casualties than they in fact suffered. The raid may seem from an Allied perspective to have been a massacre, but fierce resistance was put up and the attackers did not have everything their own way.

One member of the attacking force, who flew from the carrier *Soryu*, gave the Japanese version of events.

JUZO MORI, IMPERIAL JAPANESE NAVY

The assigned objectives of the *Soryu* bombers were the American battleships, which we expected to find anchored along the wharf of the Oahu Naval Arsenal. We dropped in for our attack at high speed and low altitude and, when I was almost in position to release my own torpedo, I realized that the enemy warship toward which I was headed was not a battleship at all, but a cruiser. My flight position was directly behind Lieutenant Nagai, and we flew directly over Oahu Island before descending for our attack.

Lieutenant Nagai continued his torpedo run against the cruiser, despite our original plan to attack the enemy battleships. However, I did not expect to survive this attack, since I and all the other pilots anticipated heavy enemy resistance. If I were going to die, I thought, I wanted to know that I had torpedoed at least an American battleship.

The attack of the *Soryu*'s planes was met with intense anti-aircraft fire from the enemy fleet, since the bombing waves from the *Akagi* and the *Kaga* had already passed over. My bomber shook and vibrated from the impact of enemy machine-gun bullets and shrapnel. Despite my intention of swinging away from the cruiser, now dead ahead of my plane – and attacking the group of battleships anchored near Ford Island, I was forced to fly directly into a murderous rain of anti-aircraft fire.

Because of this and the surrounding topography, I flew directly over the enemy battleships along Ford Island, and then banked into a wide left turn. The anti-aircraft fire did not seem to affect the plane's performance, and I chose as my new objective a battleship anchored some distance from the main group of vessels which were at the moment undergoing torpedo attack from the *Soryu*'s planes. The warship separated from the main enemy group appeared to be the only battleship yet undamaged.

I swung low and put my plane into satisfactory torpedoing position. It was imperative that my bombing approach be absolutely correct, as I had been warned that the harbor depth was no more than 34ft. The slightest deviation in speed or height would send the released torpedo plunging into the sea-bottom, or jumping above the water, and all our effort would go for naught.

By this time I was hardly conscious of what I was doing – I was reacting from habit instilled by long training, moving like an automaton.

'Three-thousand feet! Twenty-five hundred feet! Two-thousand feet!'

Suddenly the battleship appeared to have leaped forward directly in front of my speeding plane; it towered ahead of the bomber like a great mountain peak.

'Prepare for release . . . Stand by!'

'Release torpedo!'

All this time I was oblivious of the enemy's anti-aircraft fire and the distracting thunder of my plane's motor. I concentrated on nothing but the approach and the torpedo release. At the right moment I pulled back on the release with all my strength. The plane lurched and faltered as anti-aircraft fire struck the wings and fuselage; my head snapped back and I felt as though a heavy beam had struck against my head.

'But . . . I've got it! A perfect release!'

And the plane is still flying! The torpedo will surely hit its target; the release was exact. At that instant I seemed to come to my senses and became aware of my position and of the flashing tracers and shells of the enemy's defensive batteries.

After launching the torpedo, I flew directly over the enemy battleship and again swung into a wide, circling turn. I crossed over the southern tip of Ford Island.

To conceal the position of our carrier, as we had been instructed to do, I turned again and took a course due south, directly opposite the *Soryu's* true position, and pushed the plane to its maximum speed.

Now that the attack was over, I was acutely conscious that the enemy anti-aircraft fire was bracketing and smashing into my bomber. The enemy shells appeared to be coming from all directions, and I was so frightened that before I left the target area my clothes were soaking with perspiration.

In another few moments the air was clear. The enemy shells had stopped. Thinking that now I had safely escaped, and could now return to the carrier, I began to turn to head back to the *Soryu*. Suddenly there was an enemy plane directly in front of me!

As my plane, the Type 97 carrier-based attack bomber, was armed only with a single rearward-firing 7.7mm machine gun, it was almost helpless in aerial combat. I thought that surely this time my end had come.

As long as I was going to die, I reasoned, I would take the enemy plane with me to my death. I swung the bomber over hard and headed directly for the enemy aircraft, the pilot of which appeared startled at my manoeuvre, and fled! Is this really, I questioned, what is called war?

The speed and intensity of the Japanese advance through Malaya simply overwhelmed the defenders, and the capture of the 'impregnable' fortress of Singapore in February 1942 proved to be the greatest disaster in British military history. This was made possible, the previous December, when Japanese aircraft sank the two battleships sent from Britain to protect the region. The *Prince of Wales* and *Repulse* had no air cover. They did not see the enemy's approach, and could not fight back except with their ships' guns, which proved inadequate. A Japanese participant described the incident, one of the pivotal moments at which the war in the East was lost by the Allies.

SADAO TAKAI, IMPERIAL JAPANESE NAVY

At 1220 hours my wireless operator informed me that he had just received a message. I instantly left the pilot's seat and used the code book to decipher the message, which revealed that the enemy fleet had been found! On the face of everyone aboard the plane there appeared excitement and joy at having finally discovered the enemy. The message read:

'Sighted two battleships. Seventy nautical miles southeast of Kuantan. Course south-southeast 1145.'

. . . It was just past one o'clock. Low clouds were filling the sky ahead of us. Fully five hours had passed since we left Saigon that morning. The enemy fleet should become visible any moment. I became nervous and shaky and could not dismiss the sensation. I had the strangest urge to urinate. It was exactly like the sensation one feels before entering a contest in an athletic meet.

At exactly 1303 a black spot directly beneath the cloud ahead of us was sighted. It appeared to be the enemy vessels about 25 miles away. Yes – it was the enemy! Soon we could distinguish the ships. The fleet was composed of two battleships, escorted by three destroyers and one small merchant vessel. The battleships were the long-awaited *Prince of Wales* and the *Repulse*!

The 1st Squadron picked up speed and moved ahead of my Squadron. Lieutenant Commander Nakanishi ordered, 'Form assault formation!' A little later: 'Go in!'

. . . All crew members searched the sky vigilantly for the enemy fighters which we expected would be diving in to attack us at any moment. Much to our surprise not a single enemy plane was in sight. This was all the more amazing since the scene of battle was well within the fighting range of the British fighters; less than 100 nautical miles from both Singapore and Kuantan.

Except for the planes, which at this moment were screaming in to attack, no other aircraft could be seen. We learned later that the third reconnaissance plane, piloted by Ensign Hoashi, had first sighted the enemy battleships and alerted all the bombers. As soon as he had reported the presence of the enemy fleet and was informed that our bombers were rushing to the scene, Hoashi left the area to bomb the Kuantan air base, to prevent the enemy fighters from taking off.

Without interference from enemy fighters we could make our attacks freely. Co-ordinating my movements with those of the 1st Squadron, I led my Squadron to the attack so that the enemy ships would be torpedoed from both flanks. The 1st Squadron was circling about four miles to the left and forward of the enemy ships and was about ready to begin its torpedo run. Anti-aircraft shells were exploding all around the circling bombers. The planes could be seen between the flashing patches of white smoke as the shells exploded.

Not a single anti-aircraft shell exploded near my Squadron. Perhaps the clouds hid us from the enemy gunners.

Through my binoculars I studied the enemy's position. The large battleships were moving on a straight course, flanked by the three destroyers. The destroyers were just ahead of the battleships and making better than 26 knots. I could see clearly the long, white wakes of the ships as they cut through the water.

A long, narrow plume of white smoke drifted upward from the second battleship. Later I discovered this was due to a direct hit scored by the level bombers of the Mihoro Air Corps which had made the first attack at 1245.

. . . I had not studied to any extent the details of British warships, but had concentrated instead on American vessels. My knowledge of the British vessels was very meagre.

. . . I was nervous and upset, and started to shake from the excitement of the moment. We turned and flew into the clouds again. We changed course while in the clouds to confuse the enemy and finally came out from beneath the clouds in attack position. This was possible because of a stratum of scattered clouds between 1,000 and 1,700ft.

We began the attack at an altitude of 1,000ft and about a mile and a half from the enemy. No sooner had we emerged from the clouds than the enemy gunners sighted our planes . . .

. . . When the *Kanoya* torpedo squadrons had completed their torpedo runs, two level-bomber squadrons of the Mishoro Air Corps arrived at a position directly above the enemy fleet, which was trying desperately to evade the constant torpedo attacks. The Mihoro Air Corps bombers were flying at 8,400ft when they moved in to make their bombing runs.

By now the *Repulse* was a shattered hulk. It was still moving, but slowly, and was gradually losing speed. It had completely lost all fighting power and was no longer considered a worthwhile target. It was only a matter of minutes before the battle cruiser went down.

To all appearances, the *Prince of Wales* was intact, and defending herself furiously with an intense anti-aircraft barrage. She was selected as the next bombing target. Fourteen 1,100lb bombs were dropped; several scored direct hits. The bombs struck directly in the centre of the battleship.

All the bombs of one squadron were wasted. While attempting to obtain an accurate fix on the *Prince of Wales*, the squadron leader accidentally tripped his bomb release. He was still far from the enemy battleship when his bombs dropped; the other planes in the squadron, when they saw the bombs falling from the lead aircraft, immediately released their own bombs, which fell harmlessly into the sea.

Ensign Hoashi's plane caught the dramatic last moments of the two battleships. Minute by minute, as he circled above the stricken vessels, he radioed back a vivid report of what was happening far below him. Twenty minutes after being hit by torpedoes, the *Repulse* began to sink beneath the waves. By 1420 the great ship was gone.

JUZO MORI, IMPERIAL JAPANESE NAVY

A few minutes later a tremendous explosion ripped through

the *Prince of Wales*. Twenty minutes after the *Repulse* had sunk, the *Prince of Wales* started her last plunge and disappeared quickly.

All pilots and crew members in the bombers returning to their bases were jubilant and flushed with victory. We happily listened to each of Ensign Hoashi's reports as he told how the burning and exploding enemy ships were sinking

Back at the airfields in French Indochina, a second wave of bombers was being readied for another assault on the enemy battleships. The base had not been able to obtain accurate information on the progress of the battle, and was preparing to launch another mass attack. However, as soon as it received the reports . . . the attack was called off.

While he observed the sinking *Prince of Wales*, Hoashi sighted eight enemy fighters racing to the scene. Their belated appearance was to no avail, for the *Repulse* and the *Prince of Wales* had already disappeared beneath the waves. Hoashi immediately fled to the protection of nearby clouds. As the enemy fighters searched vainly for his reconnaissance plane, he skillfully deluded his pursuers and returned safely to base.

This was indeed fortunate for us. Had Hoashi's plane failed to confirm the results of the battle, our future operations would necessarily have been based on the assumption that the two mighty warships had not been destroyed. Our freedom of action would have been severely curtailed, for we dared not send surface units in to an area in which the big guns of the British warships might destroy them.

The great ability of our pilots to wrest every possible mile of range out of their bombers was soon made apparent in dramatic fashion. We feared that many of our planes would be compelled to make forced landings at Khota Bharu, since we had flown beyond our calculated 'point of no return', and then engaged in fuel-consuming battle manoeuvres. Actually, not a single plane

was forced to make an emergency landing at Khota Bharu, and
all bombers were able to return to their respective bases in
Indo-China.

It was no secret that the Japanese had designs on Britain's Indian Empire
and that, having overrun Malaya and Burma in the first months of 1942,
it was likely they would attack across the Bay of Bengal. Ceylon, with its
strategic naval base at Trincomalee, was an obvious objective, and RAF
units in the area were in a state of high alert against a seaborne invasion.
When the moment came, their plan was thwarted by a single plane-crew.

LEONARD BIRCHALL, RCAF

At the end of the war Winston Churchill was dining at the British
Embassy, Washington, when the conversation turned to the most
critical moments of the contest. Was it the fall of France? Dunkirk?
Rommel streaking towards Cairo? The Battle of the Atlantic? Or
the fall of Singapore.

Churchill said that the most dangerous moment of the war, and
the one that caused him the greatest alarm, was when he got news
that the Japanese fleet was heading for Ceylon; for its capture
and the enemy's control of the Indian Ocean, together with the
possibility of a German victory in Egypt, would have 'closed the
ring' and our future would have been black.

I am happy to say that I played some part in preventing that
capture and that is how I became known as 'The Saviour of Ceylon'.

After graduating from the Royal Military College, I was
commissioned in the RCAF and eventually joined 413 Squadron
operating out of the Shetland Islands. We flew Catalina flying boats
on our long anti-submarine and shipping patrols. Early in 1942 we
were sent to Ceylon to try and help stem the victorious Japanese
who, after seizing Ceylon, were planning to strike westwards into
the Indian Ocean.

I was a Squadron Leader and flew one of the lead boats. We

arrived about noon at Lake Kaggola and were allowed to rest until noon the following day. Things were in a great state of confusion and nobody seemed to know just what was going on except that a big Japanese fleet was heading our way and it was vital that it be located as soon as possible.

Early the next day, 4 April 1942, we arrived at our patrol area at first light to try and find the enemy fleet. It was a clear, bright day with excellent visibility but the flying was monotonous – 150 miles east, 50 miles south, 150 miles west, 50 miles south – on and on and on. The day wore on and we came to our final crossover. In the middle of this, my navigator said the moon was coming up. If we did another crossover he would get a good cross fix, plot our accurate position and set course for base.

The navigator got his fix and found that we were much further south than we should be. As we began to turn for home we saw some specks on the far horizon. I decided to take a closer look when we saw more specks, which began to take form. Obviously they were warships and there was nothing to do but go in and identify them. We had just obtained a good fix so it was easy to get their position, course and speed. Once we were close enough to identify them as Japanese it was too late. We did a hurried count and sent our first sighting message to base. This message should be repeated three times before waiting for an acknowledgement.

The wireless operator was transmitting when the Jap fighters hit us. I tried to evade the twisting, manoeuvrable fighters – no use. Our fuel tanks were hit and flaming gasoline poured into the hull. Despite our efforts the fire took hold. One air gunner had his leg blown off and the front gunner took a burst head-on. The hull began to break up and somehow I managed to get the poor old bird down on the water.

We put Mae Wests on two badly wounded crew and threw them into the water. The gunner without the leg went down with the kite. The rest of us six got into the water and pulled everyone away from the burning gasoline. The gallant Jap pilots strafed us in the water. The poor lads in the Mae Wests could not duck to avoid the bullets and were blown to bits. Eventually, when we had just about given up, six of us were picked up by the destroyer *Isokaze*.

The six crew who survived, three badly wounded, were laid out on the deck and an interpreter appeared. He asked for the senior officer. I said I was and was told to stand up and was beaten – the first of many thrashings from those inhuman thugs.

The Japs feared we had reported their position to Ceylon. I denied this and then our headquarters came on the air and asked for a repeat of the message. The game was up! Beatings all round, then we were put in a paint locker where there was just room for the three wounded to lie down, two to sit and the sixth to stand.

However, Japan's succession of triumphs was about to come to an end. At the beginning of May 1942, an invasion force heading for Papua New Guinea met the US Pacific Fleet in several days of indecisive fighting that was later dubbed the Battle of the Coral Sea. Though the Japanese performed well, sinking the carrier *Lexington* and disabling the *Yorktown*, they too suffered losses and failed in their objective. This first check on their expansion was compounded the following month by their outright defeat at the Battle of Midway.

American pilots flew the Gruman Wildcat, an old but sturdy single-seat fighter-bomber that was the mainstay of the US carrier war until the superior Hellcat was introduced the following year. A member of *Lexington*'s crew described the operation of getting them on and off the vessel's wooden flight-deck:

EMIL ANDERSON, US NAVY

I thought that it was a real good system there on the *Lexington*. The planes would land, the pilot would cut his engine, a crew would rush in from the sides of the flight-deck and push the plane forward to the elevator and down to the hangar deck, or on to the forward part of the ship, where it would be tied down secure to the flight-deck. The entire flight-deck had tie-down slots built in the deck so, no matter where the plane was parked, you could tie the wings and the tail secure in case of strong winds.

My job, on the hangar deck, was to push the planes off the elevator as they came down from the flight-deck, and park them and tie them down securely. Sometimes we would hang them up from the top of the hangar deck, or bring one down that was already hanging there.

The engines of the fighters were started by what was known as a shotgun starter. You would put a shell, that looked a lot like a shotgun shell, into the starter, signal the pilot, who pressed a button, the powder ignited and the fighter's engine started. It was decided that we would save money for the Navy by rigging up a bungee starter. A cup was put on the tip of the propeller, a length of bungee rope was pulled by a crew of sailors, the propeller was twirled, the engine started. The first time we tried this on the *Lexington* (and the last), when the cup came flying off the tip of the prop it hit a guy in the head and killed him on the spot.

When we launched planes a destroyer would take up position aft of the *Lexington* to pick up any pilot whose plane ditched on take-off. The *Lexington* would turn into the wind, the [plane] would rev-up its engine and then go lumbering down the deck, drop down off the bow, out of view, and then a moment later you would see it gain air-speed a little ahead and climb up and go off on its patrol. Those that did crash into the sea would be picked up by the trailing destroyer and the pilots and crew, if any, would be put in a little chair and drawn over to the aircraft carrier. Some in the latter part of the cruise were forced to stay on the destroyers until we got back to Pearl Harbor.

Anderson summed up one of the Pacific war's great naval encounters with the laconic matter-of-factness of one who was there:

> Later I was to learn that 18 twin-engine bombers had taken off from
> Rabaul to launch a bombing attack on the USS *Lexington*. Luckily
> we had Lieutenant Butch O'Hare and another fighter plane in the
> air on patrol. Lieutenant O'Hare and his wingman met the bombers,
> alerted the *Lexington*, which then scrambled all the rest of its
> fighter planes. Butch O'Hare shot down five of the Japanese Betty
> bombers, his wingman accounted for four more and the rest of the
> fighters and the gunfire from the convoy were able to destroy all the
> rest of them. This went down into history as the First Battle of the
> Coral Sea.

Navy pilots have written vivid accounts of the realities of flying, and
fighting, from a carrier.

ROBIN OLDS, US NAVY

The Helldiver pilots, in Ready Five, had pulled on their Mae
Wests and cloth helmets. They gathered up flight boards,
gloves, knives and guns from beneath their chairs. The teletype
machine was chattering and producing a stream of data on wind
direction and speed, position of the ship, nearest friendly land
and tactical information. Pilots jotted down each item on their
flight boards.

... From the squawk-box came the voice of the chaplain, who
was on the bridge. With heads bowed, they heard his prayer for
their protection during the battle. 'There is a time to pray and a
time to fight,' he continued in sepulchral tones, 'and now is the
time to fight.'

'Pilots, man your planes!' said the squawk-box.

This was it!

The sun was coming up over Bougainville, out of sight to the east,
and its slanting rays outlined in scarlet the great carrier and her

planes packed tightly on the flight deck. Farther forward were the Hellcat fighters. They needed the shortest take-off-run and could get into the air in a hurry in case of a surprise enemy attack on the Task Group.

'Stand by to start engines!' came from the trumpeting loudspeakers high on the island. 'Stand clear propellers!' Every pilot got set. 'Start engines!'

There was a grinding, spitting, coughing as more than three-score mighty air-cooled radial engines came to life in an ear-splitting cacophony of staccato reports, subsiding into a chorus of variously-pitched throaty roars.

The din increased as throttles were opened gradually. Amazingly agile plane-handlers snaked in and about the closely-bunched planes, seemingly oblivious of the prop-blast hurricanes. Swinging into the wind, the carrier moved forward at top speed.

Brakes released, the first Helldiver rolled forward rapidly and picked up speed. Sweeping to the deck's end, she took to the air. Her defiant roar bounced off the island and was lost in the swelling thunder of the Helldivers that followed.

Lieutenant Ralph N Gunville took his bomber off the deck and headed out low over the water. He seemed unable to gain altitude and splashed into the sea. Both Ralph and his gunner got out of the plane before it sank. Just before a destroyer reached them, Ralph went under. His pockets had been loaded with gear for the life-raft . . .

MARION E CARL, USMC

On 4 June 1942, 19 Brewsters and 6 Grumman Wildcats took to the air to intercept the oncoming Japanese. Ten returned. I had a total of 5.6 Wildcat hours when launched into combat. Due to a mix-up on take-off, only three Wildcats were together and were vectored to intercept the bombers. We made an overhead pass and that was the last time I saw a friendly aircraft until I landed. The next thing

I knew I had a Zero on my tail. Only a friendly cloud saved me as I soon found out that I could not out-manoeuvre him. Later I found a Zero by itself and shot it down. I landed with eight holes in my plane. When another scramble came a short time later one other plane and myself were the only two to take to the air. It was a false alarm – the Japanese carrier and their aircraft were under attack by the Navy carrier task force.

About noon on 26 August 1942, a week after our Squadron arrived on Guadalcanal, we were scrambled with all available fighters – some ten Wildcats – to meet an incoming raid of 16 twin-engine bombers and [a similar] number of Zeros. We tangled with the Zeros and I shot down one. I returned to the field alone and was on the downwind leg with gear down when I was jumped by a Zero. I immediately dived for an anti-aircraft battery at the edge of the field, which promptly opened fire on the Zero and started winding up the gear, some 28 turns of the hand crank. The Zero broke off and headed seaward. I went after him. He did a 180 and started climbing. As we met head-on I stood the Wildcat on its tail and opened fire on a 90-degree deflection shot. The Zero caught fire and exploded on the beach. That night I was given the oxygen bottle from that aircraft.

Most of the aircraft that I shot down, 16 out of 18, was while flying the Wildcat. It was a very sturdy aeroplane, but a Zero could rather easily out-manoeuvre it and out-climb it. It took 45 minutes to get a Wildcat to 30,000ft. It could out-dive a Zero and the pilot had full control at terminal velocity; the pilot of a Zero didn't. At low altitude there was no way of getting away from one.

On the second tour with Corsairs it was possible to climb with them and to out-run and out-dive them. Most of our engagements were over or near Rabaul and we normally out-numbered them. The war was winding down in that area and a short time later Japanese aircraft abandoned the area.

Another pilot, whose experiences were typical of Navy flyers during that eventful time, even managed to include a stint of ground-war as a guerrilla.

ALEX VRACIU, US NAVY

It was while flying section lead in Skipper O'Hare's division that I shot down my first enemy aircraft, a Japanese Zero fighter, at Wake Island in October 1943. I got a reconnaissance Betty two-engine bomber at Tarawa, and on 29 January 1944, I qualified as an ace after downing three more Betties over Kwajalein. The last of these was destroyed after a long, low-level pursuit with only one gun firing part-time at the Betty, which was jinking and turning in. I notched three Zeroes and one Rufe in a wild dogfight at the first Truk raid on 16 February 1944, as part of a 72-Hellcat fighter sweep at the Japanese Naval fortress. It was a new and enjoyable experience for the F6F pilots . . . an all-fighter raid with no bombers to protect. That night, Air Group Six, aboard *Intrepid*, was forced to retire from the combat zone when the carrier was torpedoed by a Japanese Kate.

On 19 June I bagged six Judy dive-bombers in eight minutes in what has become known as the Marianas 'Turkey Shoot'. The following day I shot down a Zero, my last enemy kill, and damaged another while flying escort for bomber and torpedo planes on a record, long-range strike against the Japanese fleet in the First Philippine Sea Battle. Air Group Sixteen was returned to the States, but after several months, I talked my way back out to the combat area when I found that I was being lined up for a War Bond tour. My luck ran out early this time on 14 December 1944, when I was shot down by anti-aircraft fire on my second mission while strafing near Clark Field, Luzon, Philippines. After parachuting to safety, I spent the next five weeks with the USAFFE guerrillas and was given the honorary rank of Brevet

Major while with them. For the final week of this episode, I found myself in command of 180 men, dodging Japanese to meet General MacArthur's advancing Americans. I marched into an American camp sporting a Luger and carrying a Japanese sword. Forced to return home due to regulations, I would not be able to make the first Tokyo raid.

An RAF pilot's account of taking off from an airstrip under attack in Burma demonstrates that land-based flyers too faced considerable dangers while Japanese air superiority lasted.

FRANK CAREY, RAF

Without radar cover, a pair of well-peeled eyes can be fairly vital when alone on forward airstrips. Thus, on 25 October 1942, when I counted a horde of over 30 aircraft approaching Chittagong as I finished refuelling, I feared the worst. Sheer numbers dictated that they had to be Japs as we hadn't got that many, so with a shout alerting the ground crew, I belted out to take off. There was an awful lot of dust flying about escorting me down the runway, and before my wheels came up I lost my temper for being such a clot as to get myself into this unholy mess. Additional horror swept over me when I saw they were a hitherto unencountered improved Army 01 fighter, and I was distressingly aware that there was only an unserviceable Blenheim to divert their attention, making me pretty irresistible. My temper made me thrash and jink about so wildly that it must have helped to save me from what looked inevitable disaster. Perhaps the very crush of queuing Japs behind me may have helped too. When all went quiet, and I was alone and still in one piece, I pointed home drenched in perspiration and many pounds lighter.

From Midway onward, the US Navy came to dominate the Pacific. The Japanese found themselves increasingly less able to replace losses in both men and aircraft, while the steady capture of territory by amphibious landing brought the war ever nearer the Japanese home islands. With her air forces no longer able to match the might of the Allies or to protect the country from devastating bomber raids, Japan adopted a desperate measure: the use of suicide-pilots.

With minimal flight-training, these volunteered to fly at specific targets in the hope of causing maximum damage. To redress what was by this time a fatal imbalance in numbers, the pilots' objective was – as their slogan put it – 'One life for one battleship'. In losing one aircraft, Japan hoped to sink an entire Allied vessel and cause hundreds of casualties. The Kamikaze squadrons achieved a notable measure of success, because an individual plane was extremely difficult for ships' gunners to hit as it hurtled toward them, and the Kamikaze earned the awestruck hatred of their opponents.

The pilots themselves were not mindless robots. Many of them were students, intellectuals and idealists. They volunteered from a sense of patriotism and a desire to spare their families the horrors of invasion or occupation. One such volunteer, who survived only because bad weather prevented the completion of his mission, described the feelings of those about to fly to their deaths for the Emperor.

RYUJI NAGATSUKA, JAPANESE ARMY AIR FORCE

A strange silence reigned. Eighteen suicide-pilots lined up in front of two rickety tables covered with a white cloth, on which were set out 20 small cups and a bottle of sake. Flight Lieutenant Uehara poured us each a little sake. At last, the departure ceremony for suicide-pilots! But it was extremely simple. Formerly, the Commander-in-Chief of the Army Air Force and officers of the General Staff would honour the men by their presence . . . but by now, the frequency of these sorties had rendered them commonplace. They were small beer.

'Now,' said our commandant in ringing tones, 'I have nothing more to ask of you but to die heroically for your country. I wish you success in this mission. Let us salute in the direction of the Imperial Palace.'

After emptying our cups, we saluted and bowed low towards the south. I did not think of the Emperor, not even for one second. My thoughts were elsewhere. I looked at the wild flowers at my feet and said to myself, 'They still have the right to live, whereas I shall be dead in two or three hours! Why? My life will have been more fleeting than that of a humble blade of grass!'

'Now listen carefully,' said Flight Lieutenant Takagui. 'The enemy ships are at a 144 degrees by twenty longitude east, and 39 latitude north. As planned, we shall fly in three formations. Speed: 150 to 180 miles per hour. Altitude: 4,500ft over land and 150ft over the sea. Attack procedure: the First and Second Formations will use the wave-hopping approach, the Third the high-altitude. Nevertheless, this may be modified by the actual situation as we find it: in the last resort, you may choose your own method of attack. Even if we are attacked by enemy fighters, don't break formation. Always follow your flight leader! Now, let us observe one minute's silence. Let each one turn towards his native region. And then we will smoke a last cigarette together.'

After saluting my comrades and the airmen seeing us off, I walk towards my plane. It is about to take me to my death, a death that is inevitable and predetermined. I begin to run. Why? To reach death faster? I feel lighter than usual and in fact I am [as I am] not wearing a parachute this time. I settle into the cockpit, get out again and touch the ground; it has supported me for 21 years – I murmur my thanks to it. Never again will I be able to put my feet upon the earth. Each gesture is the last. My seat is covered with brilliant flowers; perhaps the schoolboys, with tears in their eyes, have put them there as a farewell gift . . . I am going to die in the flower of my youth. My plane is also my coffin. Fully resolved to sacrifice my life for my country, I summon all my courage. I lay my hands on the two pockets in my summer suit. I can feel the photograph of my family and the books by Georges Sand. Farewell, farewell, my family! Farewell, Georges Sand!

At precisely 0600 hours, Flight Lieutenant Takagui's plane takes off. The second plane . . . the third . . . we follow, in order. The formation changes course, heading northeast, without waggling our wings in token goodbye. It is forbidden on account of the weight of the plane, with a 550lb bomb fixed to its fuselage . . .

In spite of my efforts, I am suffering cruelly, as if from a sly dagger-thrust. It stems not from fear of death or the desire to flee, but from the realization that I shall have no one near me at the final moment. Self-respect demands that I keep my reason and control. The American attacks are like waves that beat incessantly on our shores, and I am nothing but a prop in the breakwater that strives to throw them back.

In reality, one has no leisure to indulge in meditation during a special sortie, one must be constantly on the watch for enemy fighters, which may swoop out of the clouds at any point. By now we must be within range of the American radar. If we sight an adversary it will already be too late! Since we are unarmed and have no means of defending ourselves, and since the American pilots are admittedly more skillful in battle than we are, they will shoot us down.

If, by good luck, I do not encounter any, all I have to do is skip over the waves, dive down, and hit my target. It will be essential to hold the control column firmly so as to keep the plane steady and on course when it is shaken by ack-ack fire! Even if I am hit by bullets, even if one wing of the plane is torn off, I must hang on to that stick, so as to hit the American aircraft-carrier fair and square!

No one but myself will be aware of this act. My will, written last night, will remain on this earth, either in my parents' keeping or in the library of my university. But only I can know what is passing through my mind now, during the time since I climbed into the suicide-plane. And I no longer have any means of communicating with others.

I am waiting to get a glimpse of the US fleet . . . At the moment our formations are flying through cotton wool. Rolling masses of thick cloud . . . and now rain lashes the windshield! The position is really sticky. Yet, oddly enough, I feel at the top of my form at last.

But can we locate the 38th Task Force in this weather? I am very doubtful. Our inadequate training makes it hard for us to fly in such poor visibility. What is the flight leader going to do?

Suddenly, Flight Lieutenant Takagui points to the rear. I turn round: nothing but thick cloud. Without a radio, I cannot understand the leader's signal. Takagui swings his plane round to the left. What, is he turning back?

'No, No! You can't want to go back?' I shout indignantly into the void. 'I know visibility's poor, and the enemy may still be a good 150 miles away, but . . . why this cowardice?'

Another speaks: 'He is right. Our mission is impossible under these conditions; it's better to go back and wait for a better chance.'

This chapter ends with an account by a USAAF Lieutenant aboard a B-17. This officer was a veteran of bombing missions over Japan who, in his role aboard an air-sea rescue aircraft, was in close proximity to the plane that dropped one of the atomic bombs.

WILLIAM F CLUTTERHAM, USAAF

Along with our P-51 fighter cover we experienced in a small way what the B-17s of the Eighth Air Force out of England experienced day after day over Germany. They flew in formations of hundreds of bombers and fighters. Their average loss was five per cent or more per mission. For the bombers in the Pacific their losses were the same at high-altitude bombing but for more precision bombing they were ordered to take up low-altitude bombing, resulting in a ten per cent casualty rate. This low altitude meant 500ft or lower. Ten missions meant ten planes would go down. Not real good odds.

The now-famous P-51 was the type of plane that most usually went along with us. What a beautiful aircraft. I considered those fighter pilots the bravest men of all in the Air Force. They flew for hundreds of miles, depending on that engine to keep going. If they got into an air battle they used up the fuel at a tremendous rate. Their conversation on the radio was interesting. One would spot a bogey and announce it to the rest of the pilots as well as the bombers. What confidence they exhibited. Another pilot would acknowledge the bogey and simply respond by saying, 'I'll get 'em!' And he usually did in short order. Then there was that great Republic Thunderbolt P-47. What a great monster of a fighter aircraft that was. That great big, powerful radial engine did its work in a wonderful way. How do I express my joy at approaching the Japanese mainland where anything could happen and then to look out each side of the B-17 windows and spot four fighter aircraft, two on each side. There was a wonderful camaraderie in the ranks of pilots and the air-crews who manned those planes and those that kept them flying.

There is something about flying that is so special. Yet that special feeling is multiplied when a bunch of young kids are pulling together to protect one another. I was proud to be among their ranks.

Our point of rendezvous [in air-sea rescue role] was over the Inland Sea not far from Hiroshima. We would circle and wait to effect a rescue or be ordered to return to our base which was a good 700 miles distance. We usually maintained an altitude of 3,000ft. The fighter planes would depart a short distance away and destroy trains, trucks, anything military that they found to shoot up. It was no different this day. While circling we could not see very far horizontally. There was a haze not unlike the haze we experience in southern California. When flying, one can see straight down fairly good, but horizontally very little. As we circled in a couple-mile radius we spotted a large ship approximately 80ft in length. It was armed and had a lot of radio aerials. We were in a potentially difficult and dangerous situation. The ship could have or already had reported our position, calling on the Japanese Air Force to come get us. We had to eliminate this situation, and do it quickly. I took the plane down close to the surface of the water and proceeded to make passes at the ship, firing all our 50-calibre guns. The top turret: two guns. The ball turret on the bottom of the plane: two guns. The two tail guns, one waist gun and one in the navigator's position. Eight guns in all. We sprayed the ship with hundreds of bullets, some of them tracers that would start fires when they hit gas tanks. I proceeded to make ten passes. On the eleventh pass we didn't fire our guns but checked to size up the damage to the ship. There was fire and smoke.

Our attention was suddenly diverted to another problem. My engineer in the top turret yelled out: 'Zero six o'clock high!' The Zero was making a pass at us from the rear and strafed us. I looked straight to the front of the plane and saw the Zero's bullets splashing the water just ahead. His bullets just missed hitting our plane. Praise the Lord! But now came the fight between a Zero and our B-17. It all happened so fast. I called for my four P-38 fighters . . .

In those days the suicide pilots of the Japanese Air Force were becoming more common and doing a lot of damage, especially to shipping. The last year of the war some 17,000 sailors died and three quarters of them died due to Kamikaze attacks. If the P-38s took the Zero on, would the Zero decide to ram us? We flew a wide circle, keeping the Zero in sight so if he headed for us I could take evasive action and we could have a clear shot at him. The whole scene was one of self-preservation and it came down to 'kill or be killed'. We in our plane had put the ship out of commission, but, before we could, it had radioed our presence in the Inland Sea. While we watched the Zero closely, the four P-38s had engaged it in air combat. It was like a Hollywood movie and we were at the centre of the movie. The Zero is a lighter plane and very manoeuvrable, but light because it was short on armour-plate protection for the pilot. The Zero made a hit on one of the P-38's engines, putting it out of commission. The P-38 was wounded and on one engine it was no match for the Zero. The Japanese pilot took out after the wounded P-38, shot the other engine out and probably hit the pilot because the P-38 dove straight into the water and sank immediately . . .

Fortunately the combat ended there and then. The Japanese Zero climbed out of the area and went west. That was the last we saw of him. We were not needed there for rescue work so we were ordered to return to base.

We were 700 miles from Okinawa where the P-38s were based and it was the same distance to Ieshima. The P-38s were low on fuel and there was a potentially dangerous situation for them. Flying air-to-air combat really depletes the fuel. We didn't have a fuel problem but we found ourselves alone to return to base. The P-38s said so-long and advised us that we were now on our own. The threat was not over yet. Alone we had 200 miles to fly over the Japanese mainland before we ever arrived to open sea. We didn't know if we would encounter more Zeroes.

On the way I took the plane down to just above the water. We reasoned that if a Zero took us on he would have to come straight at us from a level position. In that position we had a good chance of getting him, because if he did he wouldn't have enough altitude to pull out before hitting the water. We felt reasonably safe. If he didn't mind dying he could ram us, possibly before we could evade his actions. Also we had several guns we could train on him . . .

We were not out of the woods yet. Departing the Inland Sea was a narrow place where the land on the right and on the left came within four or five miles of each other. We knew that there were anti-aircraft batteries guarding the inlet to the sea. We flew down on the deck so that, if they shot at us, their shells would fall on their own land. Well the upshot of the whole matter is that we returned to home base without further incident . . .

On another mission:

As we flew along toward the Japanese mainland we didn't encounter fighter aircraft, but as we broke out of the clouds there was an armada of ships directly below.

The ships were sending up flak, causing some stress among crew members as could be expected. One never knew when a large piece would come flying through the fuselage, striking one or more crewmen and doing whatever damage and injury to personnel and aircraft. A piece through the wing hitting a gas tank or controls could be costly to life and limb. It is a strange feeling that I never got accustomed to, knowing that the enemy was bent on killing me. But something was different that none of us in the flight had come across before. Not only was the black flak filling the sky, but it looked like the fourth of July when the rockets would burst and the plume would get the attention of the onlookers.

There were hundreds of phosphorous rockets. When they exploded they would spread phosphorous throughout the flight. The idea behind this kind of rocket was that when the phosphorous hit the metal of the fuselage or wings, it would burn a hole immediately through into the gas tanks, causing instant fire and probable explosion. We passed over the ships quickly and fortunately no one was hit. Not a great experience compared to that on some missions, but then just one hit could mean death for a whole crew.

Lieutenant Clutterham's plane, the 'Billie Louise' flew toward Hiroshima, acting as bomber protection. Several B-29s were above, out of sight. The Billie Louise circled at 3,000ft. Enola Gay, 35 miles away, was at 31,000ft. At exactly 0815 the atomic bomb, 'Little Boy', was dropped.

We were circling, everyone was at their guns, then all of a sudden a huge dark cloud appeared that wasn't there before. It was swirling upwards along the sides. It was like nothing I'd ever seen before.

We didn't know they were dropping an atomic bomb on Hiroshima. We didn't know what an atomic bomb was. By the time we got home, they all knew. A whole bunch of guys crowded around us and said 'Did you see the atomic bomb?' I said, 'What's that?' We weren't really sure what we saw.

Rumours had abounded about 'atom-splitting' and now, finally, the results of the top-secret Manhattan Project were visible for the world to see.

We still didn't realize then what the implications were. We finally understood what it was on the 8th when we flew over Hiroshima, a hundred feet off the ground. Like Tibbetts said when he saw the explosion – 'I think this is the end of the war' – we had the same opinion. It was just utter devastation. Of something like 76,000 buildings, only 6,000 were standing.

The problem with the Enola Gay was that it was called a flight of vengeance, that we were trying to take their culture away from them. Some people in Washington today are feeding people the lie that we were the aggressors. But Japan was trying to take over India, the Far East, even the United States. They were the aggressors, not us. President Truman was absolutely right in making the decision to use the bomb. It saved many US lives, many Japanese lives. It saved millions!

The rationale in Washington was clear: the United States had lost 250,000 men in Europe and the Pacific, and another million casualties were expected from a conventional invasion of Japan planned later that year.

If we had kept bombing using conventional weapons, we would have killed many more people than those killed at Hiroshima and Nagasaki. It was a blessing in a way, to stop the killing of so many on both sides.

GLOSSARY

Airframe	The superstructure of an aircraft.
Ball-turret	Semi-spherical gun turret used on some types of heavy bomber, with an all-around vision and manoeuvre. Positioned above or below the fuselage.
Bandit	Enemy aircraft.
Bar	In Britain and the Commonwealth, a metal strip worn across the ribbon of a medal to show that it had been awarded for a second or subsequent time.
Barrel-roll	A horizontal, spiralling roll of 360 degrees undertaken in powered flight.
Bogey	Sighted enemy aircraft.
Bounce (verb)	To attack an aircraft or formation without being seen.
Blitzkrieg	'Lightning war' or 'flash war'. German tactic by which her armed forces overran a number of neutral or hostile countries. It involved attack by highly mobile (usually armoured) ground forces, preceded by waves of bombers and often paratroops, which destroyed or secured strategic targets ahead of the main force.
'Break right/left'	Instant turn to right or left. A defensive measure when suddenly attacked by other aircraft.
Chaff	Strips of foil dropped in clouds by bombers to confuse enemy radar by concealing the shape and size of an approaching force.
Chin-turret	Gun-position beneath the nose of a heavy bomber.
Cone (verb)	To catch a plane in a pyramid of searchlight beams so that it becomes a clear target for anti-aircraft fire.

Ditch (verb)	To abandon an aircraft, or make an emergency landing, in water.
Dive brakes	Device to enable a bomber to make steep dives without gaining excessive speed.
Dogfight	Aerial combat between opposing fighters.
Drop tanks	Auxiliary fuel-tanks designed to be jettisoned when empty. Greatly increased the range of aircraft.
Eagle Squadrons	Three RAF squadrons recruited from American pilots before the United States entered the war.
Feather (verb)	To keep control of damaged engines by changing the setting of the propellor blades.
Finger Four	A flying formation copied by RAF fighter pilots from their German opponents during the Battle of Britain. Four aircraft flying in two pairs, about 200 yards apart and often at different heights, with the leaders on the inside and their wingmen slightly behind them on the outside to provide reconnaissance and protection. A highly effective positioning.
Flak	Anti-aircraft fire.
GCI	Ground Controlled Interception. Planes directed toward enemy aircraft by radio from a position on the ground
Gee	A navigational aid by which ground stations transmitted VHF pulses. The pauses between these indicated the position of aircraft.
Geschwader	The German term for a wing.
H2S	A system for radar-mapping.
Jump (verb)	To attack airborne enemy planes by surprise.
Leading edge	The front edge of a wing.
Luftwaffe	Literally 'air arm' or 'air weapon'. The German air force, established in 1935.
Main plane	Wing, as opposed to a tailplane.
Mission	An organised raid on a pre-decided objective.

Nacelle	Protective cowling on an engine or other specific part of an aircraft.
Norden Sight	US optical bombsight, introduced in 1941 and used for high-altitude bombing.
OKL	Oberkommando der Luftwaffe. German Airforce High Command.
O'clock	Position of enemy aircraft when spotted. Identified by position on an imaginary clock face.
Probable	Classification for an enemy aircraft damaged but whose destruction has not been witnessed.
Prop-wash	Slip-stream.
Recce	Reconnaissance patrol.
Rhubarb	A harassing flight in which aircraft overfly enemy territory looking for opportunity targets.
Rottenflieger	German term for wingman.
Scramble	To get an aircraft, or group of aircraft, quickly into the air.
Sortie	A single flight by an individual plane as part of a mission. A mission, such as protecting the Dunkirk evacuation, might involve each pilot flying several sorties in the space of a day.
Split-ess	An aerobatic defensive manoeuvre by which a plane half-rolls onto its back, dives toward the ground and levels off.
Strafe (verb)	To dive at targets on the ground and attack them with machine gun fire.
Terminal velocity	The highest speed that can be reached by an aircraft.
Tour	A prescribed period of duty in a particular place.
Torque	Turning motion, in this case the force of turning propellors.

Tracer	Ammunition that leaves brightly-coloured, highly-visible trails. Vivid in the memory of all who flew bombing-missions.
Vic	3-plane, v-shaped formation.
Wingman	The 'junior partner' in a two-man team, his job was to shadow and protect another flyer.

A NOTE ON GERMAN UNITS:

The Luftwaffe organised its aircraft as follows:

Rotte	consisted of 2 planes
Schwarm	consisted of 4 planes
Staffel	consisted of 3 schwarms
Gruppe	consisted of 3 staffels
Wing	consisted of 3 gruppen

Biographies

Many of the pilots and air crew in this book are among the most distinguished and decorated combatants of the war, in many cases achieving high rank in later years. The following selective list gives the highlights of their military careers.

AZARRO, 'VIC' VICTOR EMMANUEL
Warrant Officer (later Flight Lieutenant)
Air Gunner
RAF 1936–C. 1966
Lancaster
MBE, DFC and Bar

BANKS, BILL WILFRED JOHN
Flight Lieutenant
Pilot
RCAF 1941–1945
Spitfire
DFC and Bar

BANNOCK, RUSS
Wing Commander
Pilot
RCAF 1940–1946
Mosquito
DSO, DFC and Bar

BARTHROPP, PATRICK PETER COLIN
Wing Commander
Pilot
RAF 1938–1958
Spitfire
DFC, AFC, Cross of Lorraine, Order
King Haakon of Norway

BATCHELOR, KENNETH STUART
Squadron Leader (later Group Captain)
Pilot
RAF 1934–1964
Wellington/Lancaster
CBE, DFC

BEETHAM, MICHAEL JAMES
Squadron Leader (later Marshal of the
RAF)
Pilot
RAF 1941–1982
Lancaster
GCB, CBE, DFC, AFC

BENISON, JOHN HERBERT
Flight Lieutenant
Navigator
RAF 1941–1946
Lancaster
DFC

BENNETT, DON
Group Captain (later Air Vice Marshal)
Pilot
RAAF 1930–1931, RAF 1931–1935, 1941–
1945
Halifax/Mosquito
CB, CBE, DSO, Order of Alexander
Nevsky

BIRCHALL, LEONARD JOSEPH
Squadron Leader (later Air
Commodore)
Pilot
RCAF 1937–1967
Catalina
OBE, DFC

BROOM, IVOR GORDON
Wing Commander (later Air Marshal)
Pilot
RAF 1940–1977
Blenheim/Mosquito
KCB, CBE, DSO, DFC, two Bars, AFC

BROTHERS, PETER MALAM
Flight Lieutenant (later Air
Commander)
Pilot
RAF 1936–1973
Spitfire
CBE, DSO, DFC and Bar

BROWN, GERALD
Colonel
Pilot
USAAF 1943–1967
P-38 Lightning
DSM, DFC (US) (3 Oak Leaf Clusters),
AM (13 Oak Leaf Clusters), Croix de
Guerre
5 victories

BROWNE, DANNY
Squadron Leader
Pilot
RCAF 1940–C. 1945 (American citizen)
Spitfire
DFC

BUCHNER, HERMANN
Oberfeldwebel
Pilot
Luftwaffe 1937–1945
Me109/Me262
Knight's Cross/German Cross in Gold
58 victories

CAMERON, DOUGLAS
Sergeant (later Flight Lieutenant)
Air Gunner
RAFVR 1939–1945
Whitley/Stirling/Lancaster
DFM

CAREY, FRANK REGINALD
Group Captain
Pilot
RAF 1930–1945
Hurricane
DFC and 2 Bars, AFC, DFM, Silver Star
(US)

CARL, MARION E.
Captain (later Major General)
Pilot
USMC 1939–1973
Wildcat/Corsair
Navy Cross (twice), DFC (and Oak Leaf
Clusters), Legion of Merit (four times),
Air Medal (Clusters)

CONRAD, WALLY
WALTER ALAN GRENFEL
Wing Commander
Pilot
RCAF 1940–C. 1945
Hurricane/Spitfire
DFC
9 victories

COSTELLO, JOHN ASTON
Sqadron Leader
Observer
RAF 1941–C. 1945
Whitley/Lancaster
DFC, DFM

CROWLEY-MILLING, DENIS
Squadron Leader (later Air Marshal)
Pilot
RAF 1937–1975
Spitfire
KCB, CBE, DSO, DFC and Bar

CUNNINGHAM, JOHN
Group Captain
Pilot
RAFVR 1935–1945
Mosquito
CBE, DSO, DFC

DANIEL, DANNY WALTER ALEXANDER
Flying. Officer
Bomb-Aimer
RCAF C. 1943–C. 1945
Lancaster
DFC

DEERE, ALAN CHRISTOPHER ('AL')
Squadron Leader (later Air
Commodore)
Pilot
RAF 1937–1977 (New Zealand citizen)
Spitfire
DSO, DFC and Bar, DFC (US), Croix de
Guerre)

DOWDING, HARRY JAMES
Squadron Leader
Pilot
RCAF 1940–C. 1945
Spitfire
DFC and Bar

DREWES, MARTIN
Major
Pilot
Luftwaffe 1939–1945
Me110
Knight's Cross and Oak Leaves
52 victories

DUNDAS, HUGH SPENCER LISLE
('COCKY')
Group Captain
Pilot
RAF 1939–1946
Spitfire/Typhoon
DSO and Bar, DFC

EDWARDS, ('STOCKY')
JAMES FRANCIS
Wing Commander
Pilot
RCAF 1940–1972
Kittyhawk/Spitfire
DFC and Bar, DFM

EVANS, (FREDDY) FREDERICK
WILLIAM
Squadron Leader
Pilot
RCAF 1939–C. 1945
Spitfire
DFC, Air Medal (US)

FINLAY, HARTLAND ROSS
Squadron Leader
Pilot
RCAF 1940–1945
Spitfire
DFC

FOXLEY-NORRIS, CHRIS
Squadron Leader (later Air Chief
Marshal)
Pilot
RAF 1936–1974
Hurricane/Beaufighter/Mosquito
GCB, DSO, OBE

FUMERTON, ('MOOSE') ROBERT CARL
Wing Commander
Pilot
RCAF 1939–1945
Hurricane/Mosquito
DFC and Bar, AFC

GALLAND, ADOLF
Generalleutnant
Pilot
Luftwaffe 1934–1945
Me109
Knight's Cross with Oak Leaves,
Swords, Diamonds, Spanish Cross with
Swords and Diamonds, Pilot's Badge in
Gold with Diamonds
103 victories

GILLAM, DENYS EDGAR
Group Captain
Pilot
RAF 1939–1945
Hurricane/Spitfire/Typhoon
DSO and two Bars, DFC and Bar,
Commander of the Order of Orange
Nassau

GODEFROY, HUGH CONSTANT
Wing Commander
Pilot
RCAF 1940–1945
Hurricane/Spitfire
DSO, DFC and Bar, Croix de Guerre
(Gold Star)

GOODSON, JIM
Colonel
Pilot
RAF C. 1940–1942, USAAF 1942–C. 1945
Spitfire/P-47 Thunderbolt/P-51 Mustang
DFC, Silver Star, DSC, Legion of Honour
(France)

GRISLAWSKI, ALFRED
Hauptmann
Pilot
Luftwaffe 1937–1945
FW190
Knight's Cross with Oak Leaves
133 victories

HAIBÖCK, JOSEPH
Hauptmann (later Generalmajor
Austrian Air Force)
Pilot
Luftwaffe 1938–1945
Me109
Knight's Cross
77 victories

HAMMERSLEY, ROLAND ALFRED
Flight Sergeant (later Flying Officer)
Air Gunner/Signaller
RAF 1941–C. 1945
Wellington/Stirling/Lancaster
DFM

HARTMANN, ERICH
Oberst
Pilot
Luftwaffe 1944–45/German Air Force
1955–1970
Me109
Knight's Cross with Oak Leaves, Swords
and Diamonds
352 victories

HAYWARD, (BOB) ROBERT KITCHENER
Squadron Leader
Pilot
RCAF 1940–C. 1945
Spitfire
DSO, DFC

HEPPELL, ('NIP') PHIL WHALEY ELLIS
Squadron Leader
Pilot
RAFVR 1939–1945
Spitfire
DFC and Bar, Croix de Guerre (with
Palms)

HODGES, LEWIS MACDONALD
Squadron Leader (later Air Chief
Marshal)
Pilot
RAF 1938–1976
Halifax/Liberator
KCB, CBE, DSO and Bar, DFC and Bar

HOULE, (BERT) ALBERT ULRIC
Group Captain
Pilot
RCAF 1939–1944
Spitfire
DFC and Bar

HRABAK, DIETER
Oberst
Pilot
Luftwaffe 1935–1945
Me109
Knight's Cross with Oak Leaves
125 victories

IHLEFELD, HERBERT
Oberst
Pilot
Luftwaffe 1934–1945
Me109
Knight's Cross with Oak Leaves
140 victories

JABS, HANS-JOACHIM
Oberstleutnant
Pilot
Luftwaffe 1936–1945
Me110
Knight's Cross with Oak Leaves
50 victories

JACKSON, NORMAN
Sergeant (later Warrant Officer)
Flight Engineer
RAFVR 1939–C. 1945
Lancaster
VC – Schweinfurt, Germany, 26 April
1944

JAMESON, JAMIE
Wing Commander (later Air
Commodore)
Pilot
RAF 1936–1960 (New Zealand citizen)
Spitfire
CB, DSO, DFC

JOHNSON, JOHNNIE JAMES EDGAR
Group Captain (later Air Vice Marshal)
Pilot
RAF 1940–1966
Spitfire
DSO and two Bars, DFC and Bar, Legion
of Merit, DFC (US), Air Medal (US),
Order of Leopold, Croix de Guerre
(Belgium)

JOHNSTONE, SANDY
Squadron Leader (later Air Vice
Marshal)
Pilot
RAF 1934–1968
Spitfire
DFC

KENNEDY, ('HAP') IRVING FARMER
Squadron Leader
Pilot
RCAF 1941–1945
Spitfire
DFC and Bar

KINGABY, DON
Wing Commander
Pilot
RAFVR 1939–C. 1952
Spitfire
DSO, AFC, DFM and two Bars, DFC
(US), Croix de Guerre (Belgium)

KINGCOME, CHARLES BRIAN FABRIS
Group Captain
Pilot
RAF 1938–1954
Spitfire
DSO, DFC and Bar

KYLE, ('DIGGER') WALLACE HART
Flight Lieutenant (later Air Chief
Marshal)
Pilot
RAF 1927–1968
DSO, DFC
Mosquito
GCB, KCVO, CBE, DSO, DFC

LANE, REGINALD JOHN
Group Captain (later Lieutenant
General)
Pilot
RCAF 1940–C. 1960s
Lancaster
DSO, DFC and Bar

LANGE, HEINZ
Major
Pilot
Luftwaffe 1935–1945
FW190
Knight's Cross

LAUBMAN, DONALD CURRIE
Flying Officer (later Lieutenant General)
Pilot
RCAF 1940–1976
Spitfire
DFC and Bar

LEAROYD, RODERICK ALASTAIR
BROOK
Flight Lieutenant (later Wing
Commander)
Pilot
RAF 1936–1946
Hampden
VC Dortmund-Ems Canal 12 August
1940

LEVESQUE, OMER
Squadron Leader
Pilot
RCAF 1941–C. 1950s
Hurricane/Spitfire
DFC (US), Air Medal (US), Korea
Ambassador of Peace Medal

LOSIGKEIT, FRITZ
Major
Pilot
Luftwaffe 1936–1945
Me109
Knight's Cross
68 victories

LUCAS, 'LADDIE' PERCY BELGRAVE
Wing Commander
Pilot
RAF 1941–1976
Spitfire/Mosquito
CBE, DSO and Bar, DFC, Croix de
Guerre (with Palms)

MACKENZIE, (ANDY)
ANDREW ROBERT
Wing Commander
Pilot
RCAF 1940–1945
Spitfire
DFC, CD

MACKETT, ROBERT EDWARD
Flight Lieutenant
Pilot
RCAF 1941–1945
Stirling
DFC

MAHADDIE, ('HAMISH') THOMAS
GILBERT
Group Captain
Pilot
RAF 1928–1958
Bomber Command, 7 Squadron
Stirling
DSO, DFC, AFC and Bar, Czech Military
Cross

MALLOY, 'BUD' DENNIS GRALAND
Group Captain
Pilot
RCAF 1939–1968
Spitfire
DFC, CD

MARTIN, ('MICK') HAROLD
BROWNLOW
Squadron Leader (later Air Marshal)
Pilot
RAF 1940–1974
Lancaster/Mosquito
DSO and Bar, DFC and two Bars, AFC

MEIMBERS, JULIUS
Major
Pilot
Luftwaffe 1939–1945
Me109
Knight's Cross
53 victories

MIDDLEMISS, ROBERT GEORGE
Wing Commander
Pilot
RCAF 1940–C. 1945
Spitfire
DFC

NEUMANN, EDUARD
Oberst
Pilot
Luftwaffe 1934–1945
Me109
Iron Cross 1st and 2nd Class, German
Cross in Gold, Golden Front Clasp

OBLESER, FRIEDRICH
Major (later Generalleutnant)
Pilot
Luftwaffe 1940–1945/German Air Force
1956–1983
Me109
Knight's Cross, Iron Cross 1st and 2nd
Class, German Cross in Gold
120 victories

OLDS, ROBIN
Major (later Brigadier General)
Pilot
USAAF 1943–1973
P-38 Lightning
AFC, Silver Star (and three Oak Leaf
Clusters), DSO (South Vietnam), DFC
(and five Oak Leaf Clusters), Air Medal
(and 39 Oak Leaf Clusters), Croix de
Guerre, Air Gallantry Medal (South
Vietnam)
24 victories

OXSPRING, (BOBBY)
ROBERT WARDLOW
Group Captain
Pilot
RAF 1938–1968
Spitfire
DFC and two Bars, AFC, Netherlands
Flying Cross

PARKER, ('BILL') WILLIAM SEARLE
Flight Officer (later Flight Lieutenant
RAFVR)
Pilot/Air Bomber
RAF 1942–1958
101 Sqdn.
Lancaster
DFC

PEDEN, DAVID MURRAY
Flight Lieutenant
Pilot
RCAF 1941–1945
Wellington/Stirling/B-17
DFC

RAE, (JACKIE) JOHN ARTHUR
Flight Lieutenant
Pilot
RCAF C. 1941–1945
Spitfire
DFC

RALL, GUNTHER
Generalleutnant
Pilot
Luftwaffe 1938–1945/German Air Force
1956–1974
Me109
Knight's Cross with Swords
275 victories

RALSTON, ROY
Wing Commander
Pilot
RAF 1930–1945
107 Squadron.
Blenheim/Mosquito
DSO and Bar, AFC, AFM

REID, WILLIAM ('BILL')
Flight Lieutenant
Pilot
RAFVR 1940–1945
61 Sqdn.
Lancaster
VC Dusseldorf, Germany 3 November
1943

REINART, ERNST-WILHELM
Oberstleutnant
Pilot
Luftwaffe 1939–1945
Me109
Knight's Cross with Swords
174 victories

ROBILLARD, JOSEPH LAURENT
Flight Lieutenant
Pilot
RCAF 1941–C. 1945
Spitfire
DFM, CD

ROHMER, RICHARD
Major General
Pilot
RCAF 1943–1981
Mustang
CMM, DFC

RUDORFFER, ERICH
Major
Pilot
Luftwaffe 1938–1945
FW190
Knight's Cross with Oak Leaves and
Swords
224 victories

RUSSEL, ('DAL') BLAIR DALZELL
Wing Commander
Pilot
RCAF 1939–C. 1945
Hurricane/Spitfire
DSO, DFC and Bar, Order of Orange
Nassau, Croix de Guerre

SAGER, (ART) ARTHUR HAZELTON
Squadron Leader
Pilot
RAF 1942–C. 1945
Spitfire
DFC

SCHUCK, WALTER
Oberleutnant
Pilot
Luftwaffe 1937–1945
Me109/Me262
Knight's Cross with Oak Leaves
206 victories

SCOTT-MALDEN, FRANCIS DAVID
STEPHEN
Wing Commander (Later Air Vice
Marshal)
Pilot
RAF 1939–1966
Spitfire
DSO, DFC and Bar, Norwegian War
Cross, CDR, Order of Orange Nassau

SEARBY, JOHN
Flight Lieutenant (Later Air Commander)
Pilot
RAF 1941–1961
Lancaster
DSO, DFC

SHANNON, ('DAVE') DAVID JOHN
Squadron Leader
Pilot
RAAF 1940–1945
617 Sqdn.
Lancaster/Mosquito
DSO and Bar, DFC and Bar

SMITH, ALAN
Flight Lieutenant
Pilot
RAFVR 1939–1945
Spitfire
CBE, DFC and Bar

SMITH, WILFRED GEORGE GERALD
DUNCAN
Group Captain
Pilot
RAF 1939–C. 1950s
Spitfire
DSO and Bar, DFC and two Bars

SMITH, (ROD) RODERICK
ILLINGSWORTH ALPINE
Wing Commander
Pilot
RCAF 1940–C. 1945
Spitfire
DFC and Bar

SOMERVILLE, (RED) JAMES DEAN
Group Captain
Pilot
RCAF 1940–1959
Mosquito
DSO, DFC

STANFORD-TUCK, (BOB)
ROLAND ROBERT
Wing Commander
Pilot
RAF 1935–1949
Hurricane/Spitfire
DSO, DFC and two Bars, DFC (US)

STEINHOFF, JOHANNES
Oberstleutnant (later General)
Pilot
Luftwaffe 1935–1945/German Air Force
1955–1974
Me109/Me262
Knight's Cross with Oak Leaves and
Swords
176 victories

STEPHEN, HARBOURNE MACKAY
Wing Commander
Pilot
RAFVR 1939–C. 1945
Spitfire
DSO, DFC and Bar

TAIT, JAMES BRIAN
Group Captain
Pilot
RAF 1936–C. 1945
Lancaster
DSO and three Bars, DFC and Bar

THYBEN, GERHARD
Oberleutnant
Pilot
Luftwaffe 1940–1945
FW190
Knight's Cross and Oak Leaves
156 victories

TOWNSEND, PETER WOOLDRIDGE
Group Captain
Pilot
RAF 1935–1956
Hurricane
DSO, DFC and Bar, Order of Orange
Nassau, Legion of Honour, Chevalier,
Order of Dannebrog

TRAUTLOFT, HANNES
Oberst (Later Generalleutnant German
Air Force)
Pilot
Luftwaffe 1931–1945
FW190
Knight's Cross, Spanish Cross in Gold

TRENT, LEONARD HENRY
Squadron Leader (later Group Captain)
Pilot
RNZAF/RAF 1936–1965
Fairey Battle
POW
VC Amsterdam 3 May 1943, DFC

TULLOCH, DEREK ROBINSON
Warrant Officer
Air Gunner
RAF 1941–C. 1945
Lancaster/Halifax
DFC, DFM

VRACIU, ALEX
Lieutenant (later Commander)
Pilot
USN 1942–C. 1960
F64 Hellcat
Navy Cross, DFC (and two Gold Stars),
Air Medal (and three Gold Stars)

WADDY, JOHN LLOYD
Group Captain
Pilot
RAAF 1940–1945
Spitfire
OBE, DFC, Air Medal (US)

WATTS, JACK VINCENT
Brigadier General
Observer/Pilot
RCAF 1940–C. 1950s
Halifax/Mosquito
DSO, DFC and Bar

WOODWARD, (WOODY)
VERNON CROMPTON
Wing Commander
Pilot
RAF 1938–1963
Gloster Gladiator/Hurricane
DFC and Bar

WOLFRAM, WALTER
Oberleutnant
Pilot
Luftwaffe 1940–1945
Me109
Knight's Cross, German Cross
in Gold
137 victories

ZORNER, PAUL
Major
Pilot
Luftwaffe 1938–1945
Me110
Knight's Cross with Oak Leaves
59 victories

A NOTE ON THE HIGHEST GERMAN AWARDS

During World War II the German armed forces received Prussia's traditional gallantry award – the Iron Cross. Founded in 1813, this was re-introduced in 1939. As in previous wars, it was given in either First or Second Class.

At the same time, however, Hitler created a higher form of this medal – the 'Knight's Cross of the Iron Cross'. This was a larger, more conspicuous version of the familiar design, and was always worn suspended at the throat by a ribbon. It was awarded both for single acts of outstanding courage and for accumulated excellence – for example a high tally of 'kills' achieved by a fighter pilot.

To reward continued bravery by those who already had the Knight's Cross, a number of 'accessories' were introduced in 1941. These, roughly equivalent to the 'bars' on British medals, were treated as if they were medals in themselves: elaborately boxed and accompanied by citations, they were presented with some ceremony, often by Hitler himself.

1. OAK LEAVES: A pair of small silver leaves, worn attached to the medal's ribbon-loop.

2. SWORD AND OAK LEAVES: The leaves with a tiny pair of crossed silver swords immediately below them.

3. DIAMONDS: This award – the highest available to German combatants – consisted of the silver swords and leaves set with diamonds. Only 28 were won, of which several went to Luftwaffe pilots such as Galland, Hartmann and Marseilles. In 1944 an even more illustrious variant was established by Hitler – the swords and oak leaves in gold with diamonds, but only one set of these was awarded, to Luftwaffe ace Hans-Ulrich Rudel, before the end of the war.

German pilots and other servicemen can often by seen in photographs wearing the Knight's Cross and the additional awards, which are also frequently mentioned in German accounts and biographies.

Acknowledgments

I would like to thank the following people for their kind assistance with this project: Mr Emil Anderson, Colorado, USA; Mr William F Clutterham, California, USA and Mr Donald Patrick Finn, Chicago, USA. I am indebted to Colin Babb of the Naval Institute Press at Annapolis and to Eileen Simon of the Veterans' History Project at the Library of Congress in Washington DC, who gave so generously of her time and expertise. I would also particularly like to thank Squadron Leader SA Booker for so kindly allowing me to quote from his memoirs and Winston Ramsey, Publisher of *After the Battle*, for permission to quote Howard Squire's recollections. I also owe considerable gratitude to my erstwhile colleagues in the Department of Printed Books at the Imperial War Museum and to Tony Richards of the Department of Documents, whose unfailing good nature has been much appreciated.

Sources

All material for this book has been taken from a set of unique pilot biographies compiled by the Military Gallery, Wedover, with the exception of the following:

Ackerson, DR extract on 105, 107, 109, 113 courtesy of the Imperial War Museum. Anderson, Emil extract on 19, 201–202 courtesy of US Library of Congress. Booker, SA extract on 91–93 courtesy of the Imperial War Museum. Eichel-Schreiber, Diethelm extract on 144–145 courtesy of the Imperial War Museum. Fedotova, Katerina extract on 15, 149, 150, 151 appears in *Night Witches*, Bruce Myles, Mainstream Publishing, 1981. Flekser, Nathaniel extract on 17, 135–137 courtesy of the Imperial War Museum. Freeman, WJ extract on 148 courtesy of the Imperial War Museum. Gentile, DS extract on 167 courtesy of the Imperial War Museum. Hans-Eberhard extract on 52–53 courtesy of the Imperial War Museum. Knocke, Heinz extract on 61, 62–63, 64 65 appears in *I Flew for the Führer*, Hans Knocke, Evans Bros, London 1953. Mundell, Donald F extract on 19, 109,112, 117–119 courtesy of the Imperial War Museum. Price, Arthur W extract on 191, 192–193, 194–195, 196–197, 198–199 appears in *Zero*, M Okumiya and J Horikoshi, EP Dutton and Co., New York 1956. Nagatsuka, Ryuji extract on 208, 209, 210, 211 appears in *I was a Kamakaze*, Ryuji Nagatsuka, Macmillan, USA 1972. Schudak, Erich extract on 146–147 courtesy of the Imperial War Museum. Smith, Donald H extract on 105, 109, 110, 111, 112, 113, 115, 116–117, 119–120, 121, 122 courtesy of the Imperial War Museum. Squire, Howard extract on 61 reproduced from *After the Battle* No 46 with kind permission. Zuber, Joan extract on 188–189, 191 appears in *The Children of Battleship Row: Pearl Harbor 1940-41*, Joan Earle. Published by RDR Books (www.rdrbooks.com)

SIGNED PILOT PROFILE ALBUMS

Many of the accounts in *Battle for the Skies* are drawn from a remarkable collection of signed pilot profiles, compiled by the Military Gallery in 1985 and are now available from Aces High Aviation Gallery in Wendover, which is available in four bound sets. Each profile individually hand signed by many of the greatest aviators of World War II; these remarkable and historic limited editions are unique in the world of collecting.

LEGENDARY NAMES

The four extraordinary collections contain the personally signed profiles of top-scoring, highly decorated, most distinguished aces and combat aircrew; aviators whose names are indelibly inked into the history books. These are the men who fought the great aerial battles of World War II: great leaders, such as Adolf Galland, Johnnie Johnson, Peter Townsend, Leonard Cheshire and 'Willie' Tait. Outstanding combat fighter pilots including Erich Hartmann, the top-scoring ace in history, Gunther Rall (who, but for injury, might have been), Johnnie Johnson, the top-scoring Allied fighter ace, Al Deere, Bob Stanford-Tuck, Rod Smith. Together with some of the most famous and distinguished bomber aircrew, including Mick Martin and Dave Shannon of the 'Dambusters', Pathfinders Don Bennett and Hamish Mahaddie, and no less than five holders of the Victoria Cross.

INDIVIDUALLY WRITTEN PERSONAL HISTORIES

Every one of these fighter aces and bomber aircrew has personally written their own profile notes; highly accurate biographies in their own words of their wartime activity and achievements. Written exclusively for these albums, each aviator has provided exciting biographical information, graphic descriptions of their most memorable combat, preference of combat aircraft flown, and many more fascinating details. Every profile contains a personally selected photograph; and each fighter ace and bomber crew relives the most memorable combat of his career, telling us why it has remained so vividly in his mind.

PRESENTATION PACKAGE FOR COLLECTORS

These wonderful fighter ace and bomber aircrew profiles are not only unique in the world of collecting, but also form a beautiful presentation package. With a total of 110 highly-decorated World War II aviators contributing, each of the four sets is presented with its own unique certificate of authenticity, in an album specially designed to hold and protect each valuable profile document.

For more details

UK: call (44) 01296 625681
        Aces High, Vine Tree House, Back Street,
        Wendover, HP22 6EB, United Kingdom
        website: www.aceshigh-uk.com
        e-mail: enquiries@aceshigh-uk.com

USA: call toll-free 800 528 0887
        Aces High, PO Box 1859
        Ventura, CA93002-1859
        website: www.aceshigh-usa.com
        e-mail: enquiries@aceshigh-usa.com

Index